Dedicated to my wife Jean

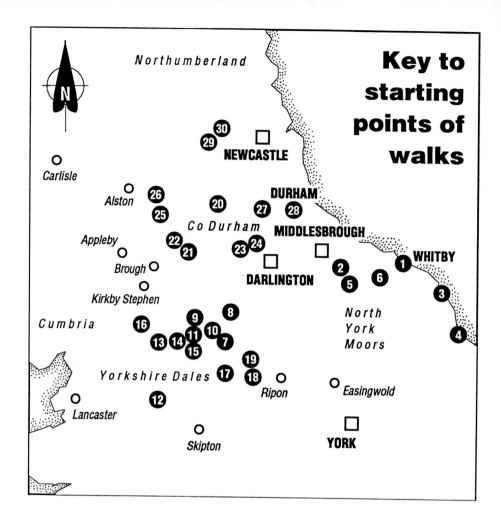

Key to starting points of walks

Northumberland

NEWCASTLE

Carlisle

Alston

DURHAM

Co Durham

MIDDLESBROUGH

WHITBY

Appleby

Brough

DARLINGTON

Kirkby Stephen

Cumbria

North York Moors

Yorkshire Dales

Ripon

Easingwold

Lancaster

Skipton

YORK

Publisher's note

While every care has been taken in the compilation of this book, the publisher cannot accept responsibility for any inaccuracies or omissions. The countryside changes all the time — paths are sometimes diverted, hedges and fences can be removed, stiles disappear.

Country Code

- Avoid damaging fences, hedges, walls.
- Fasten all gates.
- Guard against all risk of fire.
- Safeguard water supplies.
- Go carefully on country roads.
- Keep dogs under proper control.
- Keep to the paths across farmland.
- Leave no litter, take it home.
- Protect wildlife, plants and trees.
- Respect the life of the countryside.

Published by The Northern Echo, Priestgate, Darlington, Co Durham DL1 1NF
©Keith Watson/The Northern Echo
ISBN 0 9515288 1 5 North Country Walks 2. (pbk)

Contents

Colour photographs:
Cover views by David Frater
(front, Brignal in Lower Teesdale; back, Marske near Richmond)
All others by Tony Bartholomew and Andy Lamb

Foreword

Keith Watson's second book of walks, a collection strenuously quarried from a wealth of experience, can be recommended with gratitude and delight: gratitude for the work he put into it and delight in the product of his labours. The urban masses, from which most of us spring, naturally seek a recreational contrast in lonely places — perhaps wild, perhaps pretty, perhaps both. But when exploring unfamiliar or half-forgotten stretches of countryside we need to know what we are taking on, and how to deal with it. The brain, like the legs, must always be in gear. A companion like Keith is at once reassuring and stimulating: and no other walker-writer has done quite as much to guide us through the pleasures of the North and North-East.

These Watsonian walks remind me of a friend who retired in the middle sixties and decided to take up hill-walking. He and his wife knew nothing of the challenging terrain familiar to those of us brought up in the North. They needed help.

So we spent a rainy day roaming the tops around Derwent Dale. They found out about route planning and pacing and the weather, about the use of map and compass, about plastic bags for the rucksack's more vulnerable contents, and about appreciating and respecting the environment.

That day in Derwent Dale was instructive for me, too, because I had to think through — and — explain a craft that becomes instinctive to experienced ramblers. The short cut to this acquired expertise is to learn from others. In this respect there could hardly be a more caring and competent mentor than Keith Watson, not least because of the clarity and painstaking accuracy of his text and his maps. Via The Northern Echo he has already done a superb job for walkers: widening our horizons, illuminating details we might otherwise miss, and taking us by the hand, so to speak, during a day's outing. All we have to do is the leg-work. The author does the rest.

Rex Bellamy

(Rex Bellamy, who has won nine international awards as a sports writer, learned the craft of hill-walking during a Peak District youth. His seven books include The Peak District Companion and Walking The Tops.)

Introduction

Following the enthusiastic reception given to the first book of North Country Walks, about which many walkers and readers expressed their appreciation personally and by letter, The Northern Echo felt it would be a marvellous opportunity to produce a companion volume and offer a further collection of my week-to-week walks of 1988-89 which were not used in the first publication. Ten of my earlier walks from previous years have been brought up to date and are also included.

If you have savoured the fruits of the first book of walks, then you will be ready to sample this second selection which are all within the undiscovered North Country — that part of the North-East from Tynedale to Teesdale including the Durham Dales coupled with the Yorkshire Dales, Yorkshire Coast and North York Moors.

As in the previous book, the 30 walks follow recognised public rights of way. Distances vary from four to 14 miles and some walks are quite short strolls and others a lot longer, but all of them are easy to follow and suitable for most people of average fitness with moderate walking powers. All the walks are circular with convenient parking points, and public transport details are listed wherever possible with every walk. The illustrated maps enhance the text and show the route, but you will need the required Ordnance Survey Maps which are listed with each walk.

These walks will provide a fine introduction to the undiscovered countryside of the North-East and in a nutshell, the short strolls will take you to the wagon ways of Wylam; the man-made Jubilee Steps and the forgotten Fairy Cupboards in Teesdale; Wensleydale's famous Leyburn Shawl where Mary Queen of Scots was recaptured; Hawes and Hardraw Force, the highest unbroken waterfall in England, or enjoy a dawdle around Danby and see Danby Castle and Duck Bridge. The longer walks promise surprises with the Elgar Way around Settle; the Carriers Way linking wild Weardale with East Allendale and the walks from Staithes, Scarborough and Robin Hood's Bay offer some of the finest coastal scenery in the country.

May this book induce more people to get on their feet and by the noble art of walking discover the North Country. Remember the Country Code, leave nothing but footprints and take nothing but photographs.

Happy Walking.

Acknowledgements

I would like particularly to thank the many readers of The Northern Echo for their overwhelming appreciation of North Country Walks. This second volume could not have been produced without the encouragement and enthusiastic support of David Kelly, general manager of North of England Newspapers and managing editor of The Northern Echo, with assistance from sub editor Sue Kendrew. My congratulations to Mike Brough and Petra Stanton, graphic artists with the newspaper, for the splendid presentation of the excellent maps. I am deeply indebted to David Adams of Billingham, Bill Bamlet of Durham, Stuart Booth of Norton, Eric Brown of Newton Aycliffe, Peter Whitham of Hartlepool and faithful followers, David and Jacqueline Porter of Richmond, for vehicular support and being such good companions. And I mustn't forget my long time friend and boon companion Brian Hunter who cheered up a sun-soaked valley trail in Tynedale. Finally, I thank my wife Jean for her support and helping me check the manuscript.

Keith Watson

(Keith Watson, born in Ferryhill, County Durham in 1940, now lives in Norton, Cleveland. For 30 years he has extensively walked throughout northern England. He is the author of three books — North Country Walks, Walking in Teesdale and County Durham Walks for Motorists. A local government officer, he is married with two sons and a daughter.)

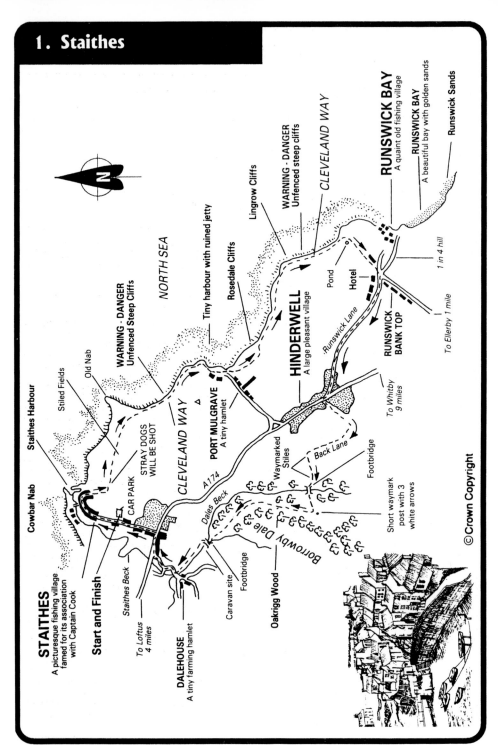

STAITHES
A picturesque fishing village famed for its association with Captain Cook

Start and Finish

Cowbar Nab

Staithes Harbour

Stiled Fields

Old Nab

NORTH SEA

WARNING - DANGER
Unfenced Steep Cliffs

Tiny harbour with ruined jetty

Rosedale Cliffs

Lingrow Cliffs

WARNING - DANGER
Unfenced steep cliffs

CLEVELAND WAY

RUNSWICK BAY
A quaint old fishing village

RUNSWICK BAY
A beautiful bay with golden sands

Runswick Sands

1 in 4 hill

To Ellerby 1 mile

Pond

Hotel

RUNSWICK
BANK TOP

Runswick Lane

HINDERWELL
A large pleasant village

STRAY DOGS
WILL BE SHOT

CAR PARK

CLEVELAND WAY

PORT MULGRAVE
A tiny hamlet

A174

Dales Beck

Staithes Beck

To Loftus
4 miles

DALEHOUSE
A tiny farming hamlet

Caravan site

Footbridge

Borrowby Dale

Oakrigg Wood

Waymarked
Stiles

Back Lane

Footbridge

Short waymark
post with 3
white arrows

To Whitby
9 miles

© Crown Copyright

1. Staithes

Route: Staithes — Port Mulgrave — Runswick Bay — Hinderwell — Dalehouse — Staithes.
Distance: 7 miles (11km). Allow 4 hours. Moderate with stiff climbs. A cliff, field and woodland walk.
O.S. Maps: Landranger Sheet 94; Outdoor Leisure 27.
Parking: Staithes Car Park. G.R. 781825 Pay & Display.
Public Transport: Tees Services X56, 256, Middlesbrough — Whitby. Bus stops at Staithes Lane End.
Refreshments: Pubs and cafes in Staithes; The Ship Inn, Port Mulgrave; The Runswick Hotel and cafe in Runswick Bay; The Badger Hounds, Brown Cow Inn, Hinderwell; Fox and Hounds, Dalehouse.
Warning: Danger — sheer cliffs. Part of the cliff path is unfenced. This walk is unsuitable for children unless accompanied and supervised by adults. Caution — cliff top path can be slippery. Not advisable in wet weather. Dogs should be kept under strict control at all times. Between Staithes and Port Mulgrave there are notices — "Stray Dogs Will Be Shot" — Dog owners take heed.

Discover Captain Cook Country with a popular round trip from Staithes, using the Cleveland Way to Runswick Bay which includes some of the finest coastal scenery in England. The return cuts inland from Runswick Bay and links Hinderwell with Dalehouse via lanes, woodland and field paths.

From Staithes car park, go down the main street to the tiny harbour of Staithes and explore this quaint old fishing village, famed for its association with Captain James Cook. Just beyond the popular pub called the Cod and Lobster, turn right up Church Street and pass Captain Cook's Cottage which bears the Heritage Trail Plaque unveiled by the Prince of Wales on June 1, 1978 and tells you that "The young James Cook received his taste of the sea and ships in this harbour village, where he worked as an assistant to William Sanderson, merchant, for 18 months from 1745".

After a stiff climb up the stepped street, look back for one of the best views of Staithes and at the Cleveland Way signpost, turn left up some more steps, walk forward and pass a farm on your right. Continue straight on along a path between the fields with notices stating that 'Stray Dogs Will Be Shot'. Proceed along a couple of stiled fields and at the third stile, go diagonally uphill to the fenced cliff edge. At the top, cross another stile by the signposted "Cleveland Way" and pause for a backward view of Boulby Cliffs, highest in England at 679 feet above sea level.

Proceed southwards for 880 yards along the well worn cliff top path, some 300 feet high with no seaward fence. Follow the Cleveland Way inland along Rosedale Lane to the harbour hamlet of Port Mulgrave with the Ship Inn 600 yards away. Opposite 79 Rosedale Lane, turn left through a kissing gate (signposted "Cleveland Way") and contour round the windswept Rosedale Cliffs with superb views of the tiny harbour of Port

Mulgrave built by Sir Charles Palmer in 1850. It was constructed for transporting ironstone to Middlesbrough and the ore came via a narrow gauge railway 2½ miles inland and through a mile-long tunnel. The ruined harbour is now a local refuge for small fishing boats.

Follow the coast path over the headland of High Lingrow and along Lingrow Cliffs (300ft) for over a mile, with no protecting fence at all, so take care along this windswept coast with steep cliffs. At the footpath signpost "Runswick Bay", turn inland, cross a stile and pass a private pond — home of the Great Crested Newt — and follow the stiled field path to come out by the Runswick Bay Hotel at Runswick Bank Top. A short detour of half-a-mile down the steep 1:4 road leads to the pleasant fishing village of Runswick Bay with its beautiful bay and sandy seashore.

From Runswick Bank Top, you leave the Cleveland Way and turn inland, right by the hotel for a mile walk along Runswick Lane to Hinderwell, where the young James Cook may have worshipped with his employer William Sanderson, who was the church warden at the local parish church. In Hinderwell, go along the main street (A174) and beyond the Post Office, turn left along the unsignposted right of way between Ivy Cottage (98) and Jasmine Cottage (102), passing Abbey Woodworkers, Oakridge County Primary School, a housing estate and along a stiled field into Back Lane. Turn right along the hedgerowed lane and where it swings right, turn left over a stile by a gate, hug the field edge and cross the corner waymarked, footpath signposted stile. Go diagonally down the hillside and at the bottom, cross a further stile, turn right along the wooded beckside and down some steps to cross a metal footbridge over Dales Beck into

(Continued on page 8)

7

(Continued from page 7)

the mixed woodland. Do not turn right, but go straight up the wood with a stiff stepped climb and at the top, emerge out into the open countryside. Go straight over the field between the growing crops, where a path has been left to reach the wooded Borrowbydale. A waymarked post with three white arrows directs you into the wood and in yards, turn right and follow the main path northwards. Keep on this and do not be tempted to take any of the paths on your right. You will pass a short waymarked post, where two paths come in from your right and continue on the main path to emerge out of the wood over a large stile by a white metal gate. Walk straight on along a rough pasture strewn with concrete and broken bricks to cross another stile by a white gate. Bear half left over the next pasture and go down the track to the hidden caravan park below. Turn right, cross the broad plank footbridge over Dales Beck and turn left along the wide track (former tramway for carrying ironstone via the mile long tunnel to Port Mulgrave) to come out at the farming hamlet of Daleshouse. Turn up the busy road with winding bends and pass the Fox and Hounds to reach the A174 at Staithes Lane End. Return to Staithes car park to complete a delightful Cook's tour.

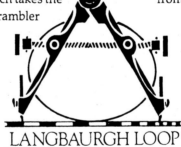

2. Great Ayton

Route: *Great Ayton — Airy Holme Farm — Roseberry Topping — Gribdale Gate — Captain Cook's Monument — Little Ayton — Great Ayton.*
Distance: *Over 7 miles (11km). Moderate with steep climbs. Allow 4 hours.*
O.S. Maps: *Landranger Sheet 93. Pathfinder Series, Sheet NZ41/51. Outdoor Leisure Sheet 26.*
Parking: *Limited roadside parking in the High Street, Great Ayton.*
Public transport: *Tees Services: Stokesley/Guisborough/Redcar; Middlesbrough/ Great Ayton/Stokesley. British Rail: Darlington/ Middlesbrough/Whitby.*
Refreshments: *Pubs/cafes in Great Ayton.*

This Cook Country walk is a classic for Cleveland folk, especially with the popular landmarks of Roseberry Topping and Captain Cook's Monument. It offers extensive views of Cleveland's coast and countryside.

From the east end of Great Ayton High Street turn left along Newton Road for 70 yards to the Friend's School, Rosehill Theatre, where across the road, go through the footpath signposted kissing gate and along the fenced path and out into Hall Fields. Follow this popular path through the fields, via a succession of kissing gates, with Cleveland Lodge on your left. Carry straight on over the Esk Valley Railway, pass the Lineside Cottage to the farm track marked Private Road, veer left to cross a stile by a gate. Follow the path by the fence on your left and climb steadily uphill into Cliff Ridge Wood, with a maze of tracks. Turn right along the well worn path within the woodland edge, cross a waymarked stile and follow the yellow waymark arrows down the watery field edge into Airy Holme Lane, turn left up the narrow lane to Airy Holme Farm, with a request "Please Keep Dogs on Lead".

James Cook was only eight years old when he moved with his family from Marton to this farm, where his father worked as a bailiff. Turn left, pass in front of the farmhouse and turn right through the faded white gate with a red painted footpath sign. Follow this broad bridleway for 880 yards along a very muddy rutted track, giving good views of Roseberry Topping. Keep on this track with notices "No Footpath" on either side and as you progress the path becomes a green grass track. When the track splits, keep on the upper path and once through a handgate you are at the base line fence below Roseberry Topping. Those wishing to climb the summit should turn left up through the handgate for a slow slog up to the trig point peak — Cleveland's most popular summit, now owned by the National Trust.

You could imagine James Cook sitting on this summit watching the ships out at sea. From here, enjoy the extensive views across Cleveland into Durham and out to the North Sea. It is here that the Cleveland Way joins the White Rose Walk. Those not wishing to climb the summit should continue along the gated bridleway which serves as an excellent by-pass on how to avoid Rose-

berry Topping, yet offers picturesque views of this lofty peak. Continue straight ahead and once through a second gate, you come out opposite the National Trust sign to join the Cleveland Way and White Rose Walk coming down from the eastern edge of Roseberry Topping. Turn right up the stony rutted track by the side of Little Roseberry with the wall on your right.

As you climb, admire the unfolding views of Cleveland's coast and countryside to Captain Cook's Monument. It's a slow slog with a steep climb at first, but it levels out and climbs again, as you wind upwards using the erosion control new path to go through the moor gate, signposted Cleveland Way and out onto Newton Moor. Here the Samaritan Way joins The Cleveland Way and

Airy Holme Farm where young Cook lived

the White Rose Walk and all three coincide with our route. From the moor gate, turn right along the signposted path marked Cleveland Way and follow the broad moorland track southwards, keeping the wall on your right by Slacks Wood. At the National Trust signpost, note the two old boundary stones on your right which serve as the boundary between Cleveland and North Yorkshire. Step out of Cleveland into North Yorkshire and continue onwards along the walled escarpment edge, noting the extensive views. After a mile, the path descends steeply down the man-made steps to the popular Gribdale Gate car park. Turn right along the road and before the cattle grid, turn left through the gate signposed Cleveland Way and ascend the broad track between Ayton Banks

(Continued on page 11)

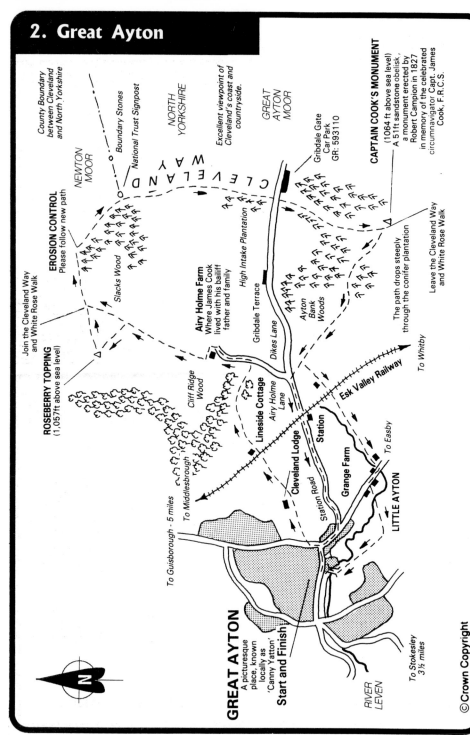

GREAT AYTON
A picturesque place, known locally as 'Canny Yatton'.
Start and Finish

RIVER LEVEN

To Stokesley 3½ miles

To Guisborough - 5 miles

To Middlesbrough

ROSEBERRY TOPPING
(1,057ft above sea level)

Join the Cleveland Way and White Rose Walk

Cliff Ridge Wood

Lineside Cottage

Airy Holme Lane

Cleveland Lodge

Station Road

Station

Grange Farm

To Easby

LITTLE AYTON

Esk Valley Railway

To Whitby

EROSION CONTROL
Please follow new path

Slacks Wood

NEWTON MOOR

County Boundary between Cleveland and North Yorkshire

Boundary Stones

National Trust Signpost

NORTH YORKSHIRE

Excellent viewpoint of Cleveland's coast and countryside.

GREAT AYTON MOOR

CLEVELAND WAY

Airy Holme Farm
Where James Cook lived with his bailiff father and family

High Intake Plantation

Gribdale Terrace

Dikes Lane

Ayton Bank Woods

Gribdale Gate Car Park
GR: 593110

The path drops steeply through the conifer plantation

Leave the Cleveland Way and White Rose Walk

CAPTAIN COOK'S MONUMENT
(1064 ft above sea level)
A 51ft sandstone obelisk, a monument erected by Robert Campion in 1827 in memory of the celebrated circumnavigator Capt. James Cook, F.R.C.S.

N

© Crown Copyright

(Continued from page 9)

Wood and out onto Easby Moor, crowned with Captain Cook's Monument, a 51 foot sandstone obelisk, erected in memory of the celebrated circumnavigator Capt James Cook FRS. The monument was constructed by Robert Campion of Whitby in AD 1827.

From this spectacular landmark, a windswept spot, admire the widespread views. From the monument, bear half right and follow the moorland path, aiming for and between the two isolated gate posts in the wall by the escarpment edge. Follow the path by the low ruined wall on your left and fork left downhill into the conifer plantation for a steep slippery descent. Cross over the broad forest drive and opposite, re-enter the plantation for a short walk downhill and out of the wood via a gate into the field. Keep by the wall on your right and at the wall corner turn right downhill

along a rutted muddy track. Follow this with the wall on your right and look out for a small gate which gives access into a small wood. The path becomes a lane known locally as Larners Lane. Follow this until you see the sign Firbrook and turn left along the unsurfaced farm road over the Esk Valley Railway to the farming hamlet of Little Ayton. Turn right along Little Ayton Lane, pass Grange Farm and beyond Holme Field and between Earlham, turn left down the enclosed path to cross the footbridge over the River Leven. Bear diagonally half right over the field and go through the corner gap and half right again over the next field. Cross a stile by a gate, follow the path by the hedge on your right and straddle a short fence. The return route is now by the sports fields and alongside the River Leven. Cross the footbridge over the river into Great Ayton to end this classic excursion.

3. Robin Hood's Bay

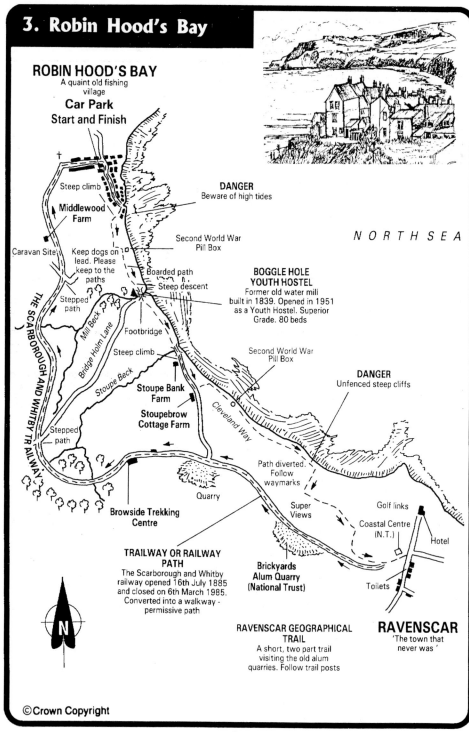

ROBIN HOOD'S BAY
A quaint old fishing village

Car Park
Start and Finish

DANGER
Beware of high tides

Steep climb

Middlewood Farm

Caravan Site

Keep dogs on lead. Please keep to the paths

Stepped path

Second World War Pill Box

Boarded path
Steep descent

THE SCARBOROUGH AND WHITBY TR RAILWAY

Mill Beck

Bridge Holm Lane

Footbridge

Steep climb

Stoupe Beck

Stoupe Bank Farm

Stoupebrow Cottage Farm

Stepped path

BOGGLE HOLE YOUTH HOSTEL
Former old water mill built in 1839. Opened in 1951 as a Youth Hostel. Superior Grade. 80 beds

Second World War Pill Box

DANGER
Unfenced steep cliffs

Cleveland Way

N O R T H   S E A

Quarry

Browside Trekking Centre

Path diverted. Follow waymarks

Super Views

Golf links

Coastal Centre (N.T.)

Hotel

TRAILWAY OR RAILWAY PATH
The Scarborough and Whitby railway opened 16th July 1885 and closed on 6th March 1985. Converted into a walkway - permissive path

Brickyards Alum Quarry (National Trust)

Toilets

N

RAVENSCAR GEOGRAPHICAL TRAIL
A short, two part trail visiting the old alum quarries. Follow trail posts

RAVENSCAR
'The town that never was '

3. Robin Hood's Bay

Route: *Robin Hood's Bay — Boggle Hole — Ravenscar — Middlewood Farm — Robin Hood's Bay.*
Distance: *Over 8 miles (12.8km). Moderate with steep cliff climbs. Easy to follow. Allow 4 hours.*
O.S. Maps: *Landranger Sheet 94. Outdoor Leisure 27.*
Parking: *Bank Top car park. Station Yard car park.*
Public Transport: *Tees Services. Service 93/93A. Whitby — Scarborough.*
Refreshments: *Hotels, pubs and cafes in Robin Hood's Bay. Raven Hall Hotel — Coach House, open to non residents, Ravenscar.*
Warning: *Cliffs are very crumbly, keep well away from the cliff edge. Check local tides before going along the seashore from Robin Hood's Bay to Boggle Hole. Please keep to the paths. Keep dogs on lead. Do not feed or handle horses.*

This splendid coastal circuit uses the Cleveland Way from Robin Hood's Bay for a cliff top walk to Ravenscar with a railway path return and both routes highlight the spectacular scenery of Yorkshire's Heritage Coast.

From Bank Top car park in Robin Hood's Bay, walk down Bay Bank and New Road to the ancient part of this tiny fishing village known as Bay Town or Bay with The Dock, with clustered cottages and sea shore slipway. No wonder that this precariously perched village is a mecca for artists and photographers.

Opposite Bramblewick's Cafe, turn right along Albion Street, follow the Cleveland Way and turn left up Flagstaff Steps with its interesting inscription for a steep stepped climb up a continous series of duckboards to the cliff top path, where you are requested to keep to the paths; keep dogs on lead and not to feed or handle the horses. Head south along this crumbling coastal path safeguarded by duckboarding to reach a wartime pillbox with delightful double views to Robin Hood's Bay and Ravenscar. Continue along this stiled coastal path and the route descends steeply down through Prickly Bank Wood to Mill Beck, a wooded ravine with a small bay which was once an old smugglers' cove. Here is Boggle Hole Youth Hostel, a superior graded 80-bed hostel, formerly an old water mill built in 1839. The hostel opened in 1951 and occupies a unique spot with the sea some 150 yards away. Cross the footbridge over Mill Beck and ten yards up Bridge Holm Lane, take the signposted Cleveland Way on your left for a steep climb up the stepped path to the cliff top. Head south for 440 yards and descend steeply again into the ravine of Stoupe Beck, another smugglers' haunt. Cross the footbridge over the beck and climb the steep paved path up to Stoupe Bank Farm with its wooden engraved name plate. Follow the lane for 250 yards and just before

you reach Stoupe Brow Cottage Farm, turn left over the Cleveland Way signposted stile and return to the coastal path. Follow the cliff path to pass another wartime pillbox with spectacular views southwards to Ravenscar perched 600 feet above sea level and dramatic backward views to Robin Hood's Bay.

On reaching a waymarked stile, you are informed that the path has been diverted, so follow the waymarks along the cliff edge until the path cuts inland along by the fenced field. Cross a wooden footbridge and follow the signposted stiled path to the end of the diversion, where a double signpost lets you know that Ravenscar is still a mile away. Pass the stepped path leading to the Peak Alum Works and at the acorn sign, turn right up the bracken path for a slow slog and where it splits fork left and follow the lane which coincides with part of the Geological Trail up to the National Trust Information Centre at Ravenscar.

For the return, retrace your steps downhill; when you see the Trail post by entrance to Peakside Farm, turn left and right to join the track of the old dismantled Scarborough-Whitby railway line, taking in part of the Ravenscar Geological Trail. The old railway (now known as the Scarborough—Whitby Trailway or Railway Path) engineered by John Waddell, opened on July 16, 1885 and the line closed on March 6, 1965. Follow this converted railway line for an easy five-mile return to Robin Hood's Bay along one of the best scenic walkways in Yorkshire.

Although the return route requires no detailed direction, you will pass Brickyards Alum Quarry, Browside Trekking Centre and follow the lovely tree-lined track, en route over a couple of roads and under several bridges. Beyond Middlewood Farm, you come out opposite St Bedes/Madonna House and turn right along the main road to Robin Hood's Bay.

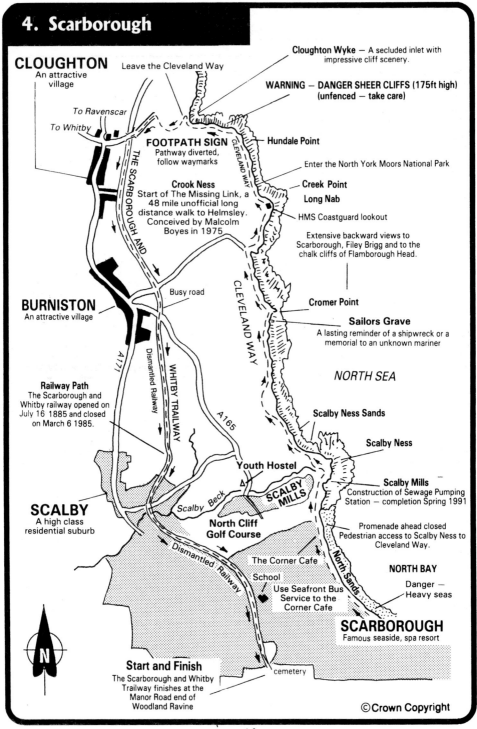

CLOUGHTON
An attractive village

To Ravenscar

To Whitby

FOOTPATH SIGN
Pathway diverted, follow waymarks

Crook Ness
Start of The Missing Link, a 48 mile unofficial long distance walk to Helmsley. Conceived by Malcolm Boyes in 1975

Leave the Cleveland Way

Cloughton Wyke — A secluded inlet with impressive cliff scenery.

WARNING — DANGER SHEER CLIFFS (175ft high) (unfenced — take care)

Hundale Point

Enter the North York Moors National Park

Creek Point

Long Nab

HMS Coastguard lookout

Extensive backward views to Scarborough, Filey Brigg and to the chalk cliffs of Flamborough Head.

THE SCARBOROUGH AND

CLEVELAND WAY

Busy road

BURNISTON
An attractive village

Cromer Point

Sailors Grave
A lasting reminder of a shipwreck or a memorial to an unknown mariner

NORTH SEA

A171

Dismantled Railway

WHITBY TRAILWAY

A165

Railway Path
The Scarborough and Whitby railway opened on July 16 1885 and closed on March 6 1985.

Scalby Ness Sands

Scalby Ness

Youth Hostel

SCALBY MILLS

Scalby Mills
Construction of Sewage Pumping Station — completion Spring 1991

SCALBY
A high class residential suburb

Scalby Beck

North Cliff Golf Course

Dismantled Railway

Promenade ahead closed Pedestrian access to Scalby Ness to Cleveland Way.

The Corner Cafe

School

Use Seafront Bus Service to the Corner Cafe

North Sands

NORTH BAY

Danger — Heavy seas

SCARBOROUGH
Famous seaside, spa resort

N

Start and Finish
The Scarborough and Whitby Trailway finishes at the Manor Road end of Woodland Ravine

cemetery

© Crown Copyright

4. Scarborough

Route: *Scarborough — Scalby Ness — Cromer Point — Hundale Point — Cloughton Wyke — Cloughton — Burniston — Scalby — Scarborough.*
Distance: *About 9 miles (14.5km). Allow 4/5 hours. Easy to moderate.*
O.S.Maps: *Landranger Sheet 101. Outdoor Leisure Sheet 27.*
Parking: *Plenty of parking in Scarborough.*
Public Transport: *Tees Service 93, 93A Middlesbrough.*
Refreshments: *Plenty of places in Scarborough. Pubs in Cloughton and Burniston.*
Warning: *Dangerous sheer cliffs at Hundale Point with no seaward fence. Can be tricky in windy weather. Cliff top path can be slippery in wet weather.*
Note: *Scarborough town map needed and obtainable from Tourist Information Centre in Scarborough.*

Early September is an ideal time for this coast and inland walk which uses the Heritage Coast Path from the seaside resort of Scarborough and offers the first hint of autumn with a bramble amble return along the Scarborough and Whitby Trailway.

From Scarborough take the seafront bus service along Marine Drive and around Royal Albert Drive. Alight at the Corner Cafe and walk along the North Bay Promenade and beyond the Chair Lift, a notice states that the 'Promenade Ahead is Closed' until the construction of the sewage pumping station at Scalby Mills is completed in spring 1991.

As directed, follow the path uphill by the miniature railway, MoD Burniston Barracks and along by the sewage construction site to Scalby Mills. Go down the winding road and cross the white railed footbridge over Scalby Beck. Note the public warning about the deep open excavations of the construction site. Climb the stepped path signposted Cleveland Way up on to Long Nab overlooking Scalby Ness and follow the unfenced cliff top path northwards for a delightful walk offering magnificent marine views.

Continue by the edge of the fields along the cliff top path for a mile to the boulder clay headland of Cromer Point with its rocky cove called Sailor's Grave, a memorial to an unknown sailor. Continue along the coastal path (100ft above sea level) for half a mile to the inlet of Crook Ness, where a stepped path dips down into a little ravine with a concrete lane that leads to the beach. This is the starting point of the Missing Link, a 48-mile unofficial long distance walk conceived by Malcolm Boyes to link Crook Ness with Helmsley which is the start of the Cleveland Way.

Yards down the concrete lane, turn left up the waymarked stepped path and at the top turn right along the field edge to return to the cliff path. Follow the Cleveland Way for another half mile to Long Nab and pass the white-painted HMS Coastguard Lookout Station. From this point there are excellent views southwards of Scarborough, Filey Brig and the chalk cliffs of Flamborough Head. Beyond the coastguard lookout station you enter the North York Moors National Park. Continue northwards by the fields with the cliff edge fenced on the seaward side. This added protection is short-lived as you round Hundale Point with sheer cliffs of 175ft above sea level. This is the highest point of the walk and, apart from two short sections of railed fence on the seaward side, there is no protecting fence at all. Watch out for this exposed and windswept cliff corner. The path descends via some steps into Cloughton Wyke an inlet sheltered by the sheer cliffs you've just walked along. Climb the steps at the top, leave the Cleveland Way and turn inland over a waymarked stile for a field path walk.

Pass a double footpath sign and at the end of the first field the path has been diverted so follow the waymarks up to the edge of the same field. Go through an open gateway and right along the next field to reach a signposted lane. Follow the lane westwards where a bridge gives access to the Scarborough and Whitby Trailway or Railway Path. The dismantled Scarborough and Whitby railway opened on July 16, 1885, and closed on March 6, 1965. Go under the bridge and follow this scenic walkway for an easy four and a half miles return southwards to Scarborough. This walk is very popular with locals for its bramble covered embankments. So be prepared to pick a pound or two if you have the time to spare.

The return route requires very little direction as you bypass the villages of Cloughton and Burniston within a mile of each other. When you enter Scalby turn left along Lancaster Way then left and right and go down Chichester Close where you turn right by the warden's house (No. 23) and go behind the flats to rejoin the walkway. In Scarborough you will pass the golf course, a school and cemetery to end the Trailway at the Manor Road end of Woodland Ravine.

N

THE WAINSTONES
Steep scramble up the rocky outcrops

Extensive views over Cleveland

Cold Moor
1,317 feet

Join the Cleveland Way
Lyke Wake Walk

Views down remote Raisdale

Alternative route
Avoids the rocky scramble up the Wainstones

Steep descent

Cairned route

CLEVELAND HILLS

COLD MOOR

To Stokesley
5 miles

Hasty Bank

Garfit

Hasty Bank Farm

B1275

To Ingleby Greenhow — 2½ miles

CLAY BANK CAR PARK
Forestry Commission — Impressive viewpoint — refreshments
Start and Finish

The Bilsdale Circuit

See the boundary stones

Steady climb

Earthwork

Extensive views of Cleveland's coast and countryside

Standing stone with wooden notice board

CLEVELAND WAY
LYKE WAKE WALK
COAST TO COAST WALK

ROUND HILL
Trig point top.
Highest point on the Cleveland Hills
1,491 feet

Leave the Cleveland Way
Lyke Wake Walk

URRA MOOR

Broad bridle track

Plaque to the Nawton Tower Estate

Signpost "To Blowith Crossing"

Grouse butts

Spoil heaps

Urra

Bilsdale Hall

BILSDALE

Bilsdale Wall Beck

Wide moor track easy to follow

Superb views back down Bilsdale

Steady climb of 600 feet up the moor

Cold Moor Lane
A muddy enclosed lane

To Carlton — 5 miles

To Helmsley — 13 miles

War memorial

School

The Buck Inn

SEAVE GREEN

CHOP GATE
Pronounced "Chop Yat"
Largest hamlet in Bilsdale

© Crown Copyright

16

5. Clay Bank

Route: *Clay Bank — Urra Moor — Chop Gate — Cold Moor — Hasty Bank — Clay Bank.*
Distance: *Over 8 miles (13km). Moderate. Mainly moorland with steady climbs over high hills. Steep scramble up The Wainstones. Allow 5 hours.*
O.S. Maps: *Landranger Sheet 93 Pathfinder NE 40/50 Outdoor Leisure Sheet 26.*
Parking: *Clay Bank car park on the east side of the B1275 road, 5 miles south of Stokesley, 15 miles north of Helmsley, GR 572035. Police warning: Car thieves operate in this area.*
Public Transport: *Tees Service 294, Friday only, from Middlesbrough.*
Refreshments: *Tea hut, Clay Bank car park. The Buck Inn, Chop Gate. Coffee, bar meals, sandwiches. Walkers are requested to use the bar. No dogs allowed.*
Note: *Do not attempt in doubtful weather. Carry map and compass.*

This high level route along the Cleveland Hills is one of the best hill walks in Britain, with extensive views over Cleveland's countryside. From Clay Bank car park turn left along the busy B1275 and in 200 yards turn left through a gate signposted "Cleveland Way" for an uphill walk shared by six well-known long distance paths. Follow the path steadily uphill by the forestry boundary wall. Pass through a gate and up a steep stretch for a scramble through a narrow cleft in rocky outcrops.

The next gate displays notices about lambing and upland nesting birds. It's worth looking back at the extensive views of Cringle Moor, Cold Moor and Hasty Bank, if you need an excuse for a pause. Stride out and head eastwards along Carr Ridge with a gradual climb on Urra Moor dotted with standing stones and round burial mounds. There is a bird's eye view of beautiful Bilsdale plus the local landmarks of Roseberry Topping and Captain Cook's Monument. Follow the broad bridle track, a cairned route over the rise and look out for a boundary stone marked 'M' by a wooden notice board without a notice, both on your left.

Here a short extension can be made to 'bag' the white trig point top of Roundhill on Botton Head seen in the distance. At 1,491ft above sea level it's the highest point on the Cleveland Hills. From the boundary stone fork right, pass a large cairn and follow the broad track south westwards across Urra Moor for one and a half miles. As you approach the moor edge, pass a row of heather-covered shooting butts (nine in all) on your right. Next to them is a recently erected plaque to the Nawton Tower Estate and further on the signpost "To Blowith Crossing". Where the track turns left walk straight on down the moor edge with superb views to Bilsdale.

Pass an even larger estate notice on your right. Cross the facing wall stile and go downhill on a slippery track that passes a ruined red pantiled barn on your right. Follow the stiled bridle track that winds left amidst evidence of old spoil heaps and contours round to come out by Bilsdale Hall. Turn left down the lane past the neat roadside cottages to Seave Green and the B1275. Turn left along the main road to Chop Gate, the largest hamlet in Bilsdale. The Buck Inn is an ideal halfway house for refreshments.

For the return route leave 'Chop Yat' opposite the War Memorial and yards along the Carlton road, turn immediately right up the cobbled Cold Moor Lane. It's a signposted public bridleway. Pass the Wesleyan chapel dated 1858 and follow the enclosed, unsurfaced lane northwards for 880 yards. Expect plenty of mud. At the top exit through a gate marked "Please shut this gate" out on to Cold Moor for a two and a half mile moorland ridge walk. At first walk by the wall on your right and leave this for a steady climb up the moor to join a broad track on the top moor. Follow this ridge walk with views into remote Raisdale and classic views of the Cleveland Hills. Continue on the rising path to the cairned summit of Cold Moor (1,317ft) with extensive, uninterrupted views north over the Cleveland Plain.

From Cold Moor turn right, follow the Cleveland Way downhill to Garfit Gap and take care on the steep descent as it is stony and slippery. At the bottom go through a wooden gate and proceed up through a couple of wall gaps to the sandstone outcrops of the well-known Wainstones popular with climbers. If you don't fancy the rocky scramble there is an alternative route as shown on my map. It is a little longer and bypasses the Wainstones. As you approach the second wall gap, fork right and across a stepboard stile by a gate and follow the path round the stiled fields by the farmsteads of Garfit and Hasty Bank to follow the farm track back to the B1275 for a return to Clay Bank.

For the main route climb the Wainstones and follow the well worn track with care over Hasty Bank for a steep, stony descent downhill to the B1275 and return to Clay Bank.

6. Danby

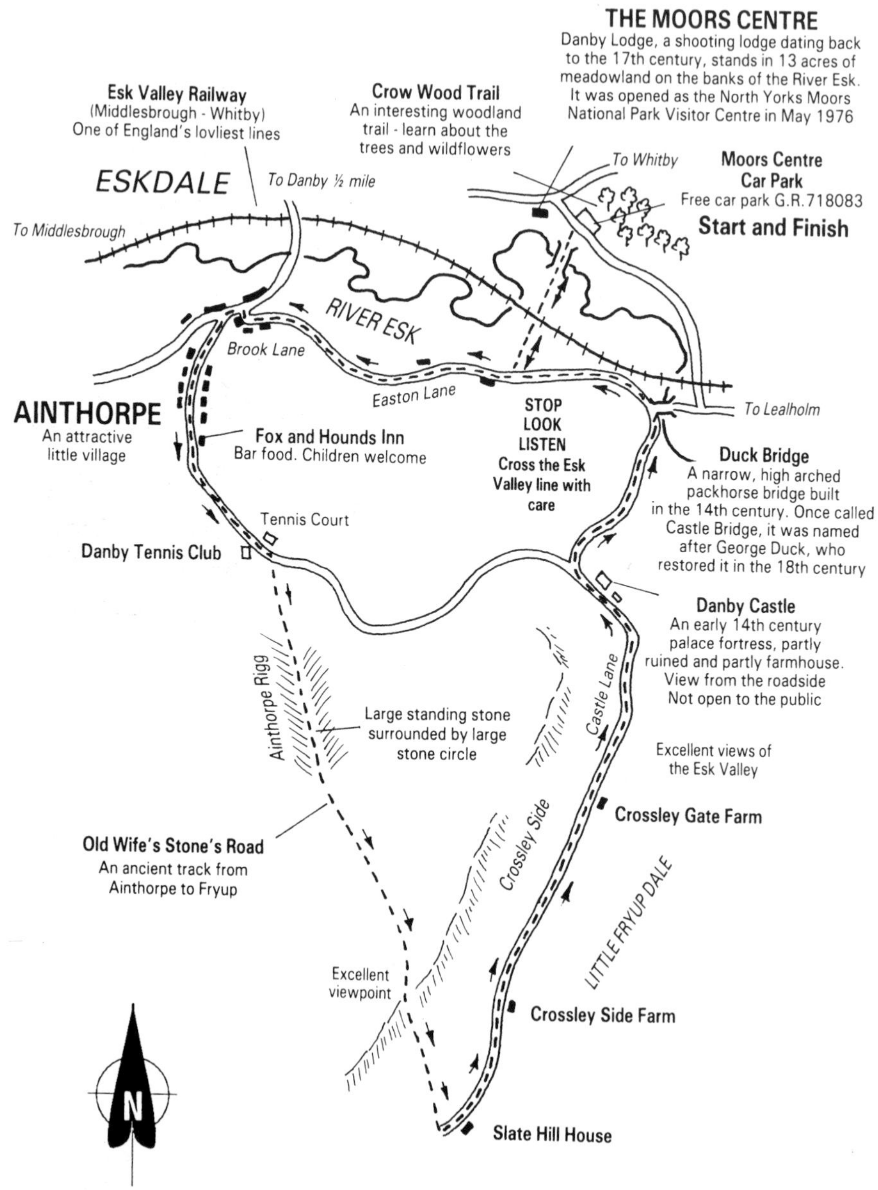

THE MOORS CENTRE
Danby Lodge, a shooting lodge dating back to the 17th century, stands in 13 acres of meadowland on the banks of the River Esk. It was opened as the North Yorks Moors National Park Visitor Centre in May 1976

To Whitby

Moors Centre Car Park
Free car park G.R.718083
Start and Finish

Esk Valley Railway
(Middlesbrough - Whitby)
One of England's lovliest lines

Crow Wood Trail
An interesting woodland trail - learn about the trees and wildflowers

ESKDALE

To Danby ½ mile

To Middlesbrough

RIVER ESK

Brook Lane

Easton Lane

AINTHORPE
An attractive little village

Fox and Hounds Inn
Bar food. Children welcome

STOP LOOK LISTEN
Cross the Esk Valley line with care

To Lealholm

Duck Bridge
A narrow, high arched packhorse bridge built in the 14th century. Once called Castle Bridge, it was named after George Duck, who restored it in the 18th century

Tennis Court

Danby Tennis Club

Danby Castle
An early 14th century palace fortress, partly ruined and partly farmhouse.
View from the roadside
Not open to the public

Ainthorpe Rigg

Castle Lane

Large standing stone surrounded by large stone circle

Excellent views of the Esk Valley

Old Wife's Stone's Road
An ancient track from Ainthorpe to Fryup

Crossley Side

Crossley Gate Farm

LITTLE FRYUP DALE

Excellent viewpoint

Crossley Side Farm

N

Slate Hill House

6. The Moors Centre, Danby

Route: *The Moors Centre, Danby — Ainthorpe — Ainthorpe Rigg — Danby Rigg — Danby Castle — Duck Bridge — Danby.*
Distance: *Over 4 miles (6.5 km). Allow 2½ to 3 hours. Fairly easy, except for a moorland ridge walk. Field, moor and country lanes.*
O.S. Maps: *Landranger Sheet 94. Pathfinder Series Sheet NZ 60/70. Outdoor Leisure Sheet 27.*
Parking: *The Moors Centre Car Park, Danby Lodge. (Free car park) GR 718083.*
Refreshments: *Tearooms, The Moors Centre; Fox and Hounds, Ainthorpe, bar food. Children welcome.*
Note: *The Moors Centre, Danby Lodge, is open daily April 1 to October 31, 10am to 5pm. Open November to March Sundays only noon to 4pm. Waymark Walks are a popular series of self-guided walk leaflets published by the North York Moors National Park. They briefly describe in words and sketch map, a short family walk of between two and five miles within the National Park.*

This short circular stroll follows the popular Waymark Walk (Number 25) based on the Moors Centre at Danby in the heart of the Esk Valley. It takes you along quiet country lanes to the attractive Ainthorpe village and traverses a breezy moorland ridge, dotted with ancient burial cairns and standing stones with extensive Esk Valley views. The second part on lanes, passes a 14th century palace fortress and visits a high arched packhorse bridge. From the Moors Centre car park cross the road and outside the entrance to the Moors Centre go through the signposted handgate and head south westwards alongside the perimeter centre fence. Cross the footbridge over the River Esk and walk straight on following the waymarked footpath sign and noting the request to keep to the path.

The Moors Centre, Danby

Aim through the kissing gate, cross the Esk Valley Railway with the notice "Stop, Look, Listen, — (Beware of the trains)". Note the past and present railway penalty fines. Continue along the next fenced field with an interesting notice "noo mind t' bull, bes naughty". At the field end, cross the corner signposted step stile. Turn right along Easton Lane to Ainthorpe village where you turn right by Ainthorpe Farm, then left and left again into Brook Lane. Walk up the lane for 880 yards, past the Fox and Hounds Inn and beyond Danby Tennis Club, where the lane swings left, turn right at the public bridleway signpost and head up the gorse-covered moor. Go through the moor gate, giving access on to Ainthorpe Rigg, and head up the ancient track called the Old Wife's Stones Road. It's certainly a stony track with small and large cairns, dotted with standing stones.

As you climb, see if you can spot Roseberry Topping, Captain Cook's Monument and Freebrough Hill, as well as the Esk Valley villages of Castleton and Danby.

Continue over the moor top, noting the large standing stone surrounded by a large stone circle, part of the iron and bronze age settlement on Danby Rigg. On the escarpment edge of Danby Rigg (1,000ft) above Crossley Side, look down on the patchwork pastures of Little Fryup Dale with views into Great Fryup Dale. Go down the stone slab staircase, on a good brown bracken track to come out on the lane opposite Slate Hill House. Turn left along the traffic free road, except for farm vehicles, and follow Castle Lane for about one and a half miles past the roadside farmsteads of Crossley Side and Crossley Gate. You will get a roadside view of Danby Castle, an early 14th century palace fortress, part ruin and part farmhouse. Catherine Parr, sixth and last wife of Henry VIII lived here. The castle is not open to the public. Beyond the castle, turn right down the winding road for 880 yards to the narrow hump bridge called Duck Bridge. It's a 14th century packhorse bridge, named after George Duck who restored it in the 18th century. Do not cross the bridge, but turn left along Easton Lane, noting an interesting warning notice fixed to a tree about a bull. When you reach the signposted step stile on your right, return by the same outward route to complete a very satisfying Waymark Walk.

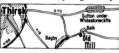

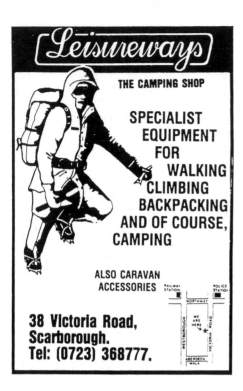

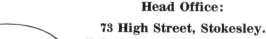

27

29

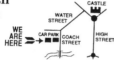

All tied up. . .traditional cobles in the port of Staithes.

Step out from Romaldkirk — and enter the Great Wood.

7. Jervaulx Abbey

Route: Jervaulx Abbey — Cover Bridge — Ulshaw Bridge — Thornton Steward — Kilgram Bridge — Jervaulx Abbey.
Distance: 7 miles (11km). Easy. Allow 3 hours.
O.S. Maps: Landranger Sheet 99, Pathfinder Sheet 630 (SE17/18)
Parking: Jervaulx Abbey car park — two miles east of Cover Bridge, off A6108 Middleham — Masham road. Warning — Vehicles and contents are parked at owners risk.
Public Transport: United Service 159 Hawes — Ripon on Thursday and Saturday only — one service per day. Check bus time tables.
Refreshments: Jervaulx Abbey Gardens Cafe and Tea Garden: Open April — October; Jervaulx Hall Hotel; The Cover Bridge Inn with Beer Garden — children and dogs welcome.
Jervaulx Abbey: Open to public. Honesty Box — Admission charges: Adults — 75p, Children 35p. The owners of Jervaulx Abbey regret that they cannot accept liabilty for injury to visitors or loss of, or damage to their property. Parts of this monument are dangerous. Visitors are requested not to pick flowers or to leave litter around the Abbey.
Note: Please keep dogs on lead. The Pathfinder map is recommended for the field path route between Thornton Steward and Kilgram Bridge even though it is well waymarked. Danby Hall is a private residence and not open to the public.

This delightful Wensleydale walk teems from end to end with historic interest and includes three ancient bridges, two old corn mills, a mansion, an old church and a Cistercian Abbey.

With hardly a hill to climb, this low level walk takes you along one of the best waterside walks in Wensleydale which combines pasture and parkland paths with lovely little country lanes. The walk is rewarded with a superb finish at the ruined remains of Jervaulx Abbey, one of the most beautiful Cistercian Abbeys in England.

From Jervaulx Abbey car park, turn left along the busy A6108 for 300 yards, pass Jervaulx Hall Hotel and immediately beyond Harker Beck Bridge, turn right through the waymarked gate with a request — "Private Property — Footpath Only — Dogs On Lead Please". Follow the beckside track through a waymarked wooden gate announcing "Private Fishing on the Jervaulx and Danby Estates" to reach the riverside. Turn left and follow the River Ure upstream for two miles to Cover Bridge with no guidance needed. This riverside path, one of the best waterside walks in Wensleydale is famous for its fly fishing (private) and was a popular route with the white-robed monks of Jervaulx Abbey. It is full of interest with views and varied bird life including the occasional heron and white swans on the nearby fish pond.

As you progress upriver, you can see Danby Hall and further on, the old Danby Low Mill by the weir. To the south is the lovely estate village of East Witton wedged below Witton Fell. When you reach the three tree-topped islands called The Batts, where the River Cover joins the River Ure — watch out for the Waterhorse or Kelpie that haunts this stretch of the river. At the main road

A6108, turn right over the humpbacked Cover Bridge built in 1766 and call in at the 16th century Cover Bridge Inn, a popular pub with walkers and fishermen. The interior of this olde worlde pub was one of the location scenes used in 1990 in the popular TV series, All Creatures Great And Small.

Outside the pub at the road junction, turn right in the direction of Spennithorne to cross Ulshaw Bridge over the River Ure. This fine old bridge has a pedestal sundial dated R.W. 1674. Just over the bridge at the road junction, turn right along the lane for 880 yards, pass the Catholic Church of St Simon and St Jude and where the lane bends left, note the derelict Danby High Mill, an early corn water mill. Go forward along the Public Bridleway, an unsurfaced track by the wooded riverside, to pass Danby Low Mill, another disused old corn mill by a neat farm cottage. Go through the park gates into the delightful parkland of Danby Low Park. Keep to the carriageway as it steadily turns up towards Danby Hall, a magnificent Elizabethan mansion, once the ancestral home of the Scrope family.

As you approach the hall, turn right along a stony track at first and aim for a yellow arrow fixed on an old oak tree. The waymarks within the parkland have been provided by the County Landowners Assocation. At the far end of the parkland, go through the waymarked metal gate and proceed eastwards in the same direction along the edge of more five gated fields with one single stile, all waymarked with blue arrows to reach the isolated St Oswald's Church, regarded

(Continued on page 37)

35

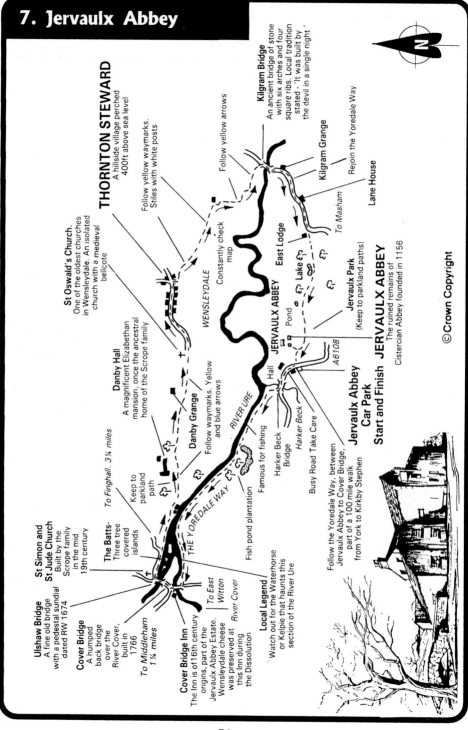

N

THORNTON STEWARD
A hillside village perched 400ft above sea level

Kilgram Bridge
An ancient bridge of stone with six arches and four square ribs. Local tradition stated - 'It was built by the devil in a single night'

Follow yellow waymarks. Stiles with white posts

Follow yellow arrows

Kilgram Grange

Rejoin the Yoredale Way

St Oswald's Church.
One of the oldest churches in Wensleydale. An isolated church with a medieval bellcote

To Masham

Lane House

Constantly check map

East Lodge

Danby Hall
A magnificent Elizabethan mansion, once the ancestral home of the Scrope family

WENSLEYDALE

JERVAULX ABBEY

Lake

Jervaulx Park
(Keep to parkland paths)

Pond

JERVAULX ABBEY
The ruined remains of Cistercian Abbey founded in 1156

To Finghall. 3¼ miles

Keep to parkland path

Danby Grange

Follow waymarks. Yellow and blue arrows

Hall

RIVER URE

A6108

Jervaulx Abbey Car Park
Start and Finish

The Batts
Three tree covered islands

Harker Beck Bridge

Harker Beck

Famous for fishing

Busy Road Take Care

Follow the Yoredale Way, between Jervaulx Abbey to Cover Bridge, part of a 100 mile walk from York to Kirkby Stephen

Ulshaw Bridge
A fine old bridge with a pedestal sundial dated RW 1674

St Simon and St Jude Church
Built by the Scrope family in the mid 19th century

Cover Bridge
A humped back bridge over the River Cover, built in 1766

To Middleham 1¼ miles

Cover Bridge Inn
The Inn is of 16th century origins, part of the Jervaulx Abbey Estate. Wensleydale cheese was preserved at this Inn during the Dissolution

To East Witton

River Cover

Fish pond plantation

THE YOREDALE WAY

Local Legend
Watch out for the Waterhorse or Kelpie that haunts this section of the River Ure

© Crown Copyright

36

(Continued from page 35)

as one of the oldest churches in Wensleydale. This trim church has a medieval bellcote with two bells which were rung to summon people to worship, as much as five times a day. The church is well worth a visit.

From the church, follow the lane for 880 yards up the only hill climb on the walk to the hillside village of Thornton Steward, perched 400 feet above sea level with extensive views of lower Wensleydale. Pass through this tiny village with a Manor House, neat cottages and an old school erected A.D. 1866. The field path route from Thornton Steward to Kilgram Bridge, starts opposite the school and is fairly easy to follow eastwards along the stiled fields, waymarked with yellow arrows and white posts. You might encounter a couple of securely tied gates, especially one, a field away from Woodhouse Farm. The use of the O.S. Pathfinder Map is recommended and should be constantly checked as you progess eastwards down to Kilgram Bridge.

Kilgram Bridge, a great old bridge, is said to have been built by the Devil in a night. Cross the bridge over the River Ure and follow the narrow Kilgram Lane for 880 yards to reach East Lodge and enter Jervaulx Park for another delightful parkland walk. Keep to the carriageway, pass the lake and pond to reach the silent splendour of the ruined Jervaulx Abbey founded in 1156. A fitting climax and superb finish for one of the best walks in Wensleydale.

8. Richmond

8. Richmond

Route: Richmond — Billy Bank Wood — Round Howe — Calfhall Wood — Hudswell — Round Howe — Richmond.
Distance: Over 5 miles (8km). Easy with a steep climb. Allow 2/3 hours.
O.S. Maps: Landranger Sheet 92. Pathfinder Sheet 609 (NZ10/SE19).
Parking: Market Place, Richmond.
Public Transport: Richmond is served by United Services from Darlington, Catterick, Northallerton, Hawes and Keld.
Refreshments: Pubs, hotels, cafes in Richmond; George and Dragon, Hudswell.
Note: Please keep to the wood and riverside paths.

This popular woodland riverside ramble is one of the best walks around Richmond in beautiful Swaledale. Leave Richmond Market Place by the New Road and in yards, bear left down the narrow lane called The Bar. Go under the postern gate and descend the steep cobbled Cornforth Hill to come out opposite the Oak Tree pub. Walk down Bridge Street and cross Green Bridge over the River Swale, noting the inscribed panel with distances Askrigg 18 miles: Lancaster 56 miles.

At the foot of Sleegill, turn right and go between the corner cottage and the bridge into Billy Bank Wood. Follow the broad woodland, riverside path and look back for the best views of the bridge and castle. After 150 yards, a path branches off to the right which is the riverside return route. Stay on the main path and take the railed stone steps by the rocky outcrops, strewn with huge stone slabs, for a short steep climb on a stony path up through the delightful woodland. Do not go to the top of the woodland, but branch right on a level path that leads down to a railed bridge over a dry gulley. A National Trust sign fixed to the rock face indicates that you are now in Hudswell Woods.

Ignore the stepped path down to the river. The main path descends through the splendid wood to cross a stile by another National Trust sign. Turn left along the riverside meadow by the wood and as you walk westwards, look out for the half hidden, natural cave called King Arthur's Oven. At the end of the first field cross a waymarked stile, fork half right and join the riverside path, where you will see a tree-covered conical hill, aptly named Round Howe. On reaching the metal footbridge which spans the Swale there is a picnic area on the north bank of the river which is a good spot for a stop. Pass the bridge and continue westwards into Calfhall Wood. Cross a stile and the path drops down some steep railed steps to the river's edge with charming views of the Swale. The path can be very muddy even in summer and the rocks very slippery in wet weather. After a mile, the path leaves the river and branches half left to emerge out of the wood at a public footpath sign situated above the pumping station. Turn left and climb the steep steps, 328 of them, made by German prisoners during the Second World War to link the pumping station with the treatment plant above. Do take your time to climb these steps, illuminated by street lamps. Pause now and again to get your breath back and admire the westward views over lower Swaledale to Whitcliffe Scar and Willance's Leap.

At the double footpath sign, you can turn left along the top of Calfhall Wood or if in need of refreshments, climb the final set of steps, cross the stile and follow the path up the field edge to come out opposite Orana, in the hilltop village of Hudswell, where the George and Dragon offers good meals. Children are welcome here providing they are well behaved. From the pub, turn left along the village street and just beyond the old school look out for a wooden footpath sign fixed to the wall between Random House and Norley. Go along the short walled lane and down the field to cross a concealed metal stile by a gate. Bear left alongside the railed fence to join the path that has come from the steep steps. Turn right along the level path above Calfhall Wood, cross a dry watercourse and over a stile. Keep along the woodland edge until the path ends at half a dozen wooden steps. Climb these, cross a stile and turn left along the field edge until a stile in the same field admits you back into the woodland. Again, keep along the top of the wood and ignore a stile on your right. Follow the railed rough path down to a stile and exit out of the wood.

Walk forward, join a rutted track for a pleasant downhill walk with excellent eastward views of Richmond. The track winds down fairly steeply, past an old oak tree with a public footpath sign fixed to it. Continue down to go under the tree branches to come out almost opposite the metal footbridge at Round Howe. You'll find yourself back on the outward route and bear left over a waymarked stile by an open gate. Follow the lovely riverside path for the best part of the walk. This pleasant stretch of riverside is very popular with local people. At the far end of the riverside meadow cross a stile into an enclosed path under Billy Bank Wood and walk along the great limestone slabs which formed a cart track used by horses and carts from the nearby Billy Bank copper mine. If the river is low, continue on for some boulder hopping to rejoin the outward route to complete an interesting woodland walk.

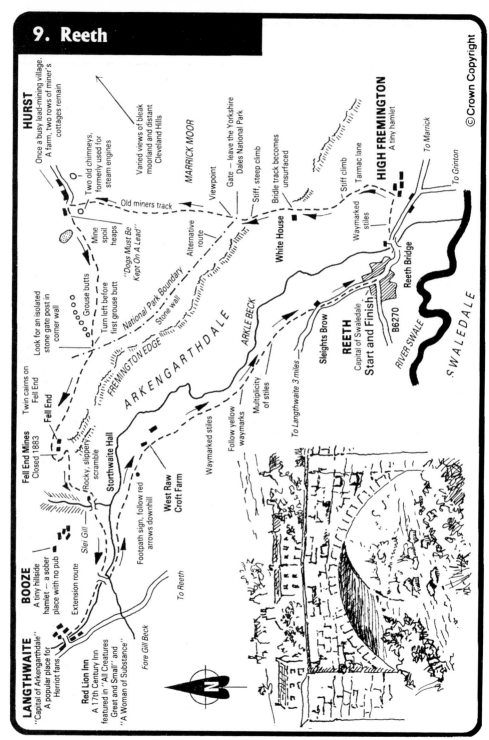

HURST
Once a busy lead-mining village. A farm, two rows of miner's cottages remain

Two old chimneys, formerly used for steam engines

Varied views of bleak moorland and distant Cleveland Hills

MARRICK MOOR

Viewpoint

Gate – leave the Yorkshire Dales National Park

Stiff, steep climb

Bridle track becomes unsurfaced

Stiff climb

Tarmac lane

HIGH FREMINGTON
A tiny hamlet

To Marrick

To Grinton

Old miners track

Mine spoil heaps

"Dogs Must Be Kept On A Lead"

Alternative route

Waymarked stiles

White House

Reeth Bridge

B6270

Grouse butts

Turn left before first grouse butt

National Park Boundary

Stone wall

FREMINGTON EDGE

ARKENGARTHDALE

ARKLE BECK

RIVER SWALE

S W A L E D A L E

Look for an isolated stone gate post in corner wall

Twin cairns on Fell End

Fell End

Fell End Mines
Closed 1883

Rocky, slippery scramble

Storthwaite Hall

West Raw Croft Farm

Waymarked stiles

Sleights Brow

REETH
Capital of Swaledale
Start and Finish

Multiplicity of stiles

Follow yellow waymarks

To Langthwaite 3 miles

Footpath sign, follow red arrows downhill

Slei Gill

BOOZE
A tiny hillside hamlet — a sober place with no pub

Extension route

LANGTHWAITE
"Capital of Arkengarthdale"
A popular place for Herriot fans

Red Lion Inn
A 17th Century Inn featured in "All Creatures Great and Small" and "A Woman of Substance"

To Reeth

Fore Gill Beck

N

9. Reeth

Route: Reeth — High Fremington — Fremington Edge — Hurst — Fell End —
Langthwaite — West Raw Croft Farm — Reeth.
Distance: About 8 miles (13km). Allow 4/5 hours. Moderate. A couple of stiff climbs.
Moorland and field paths.
Parking: On the cobbled area of The Green, Reeth.
Public Transport: United Services 30, Richmond to Keld.
Refreshments: Plenty of pubs and cafes in Reeth. Red Lion Inn, Langthwaite.
Note: Expect high winds on the exposed Fremington Edge.

An airy upland walk of eight miles around Reeth in Swaledale offering superb aerial views of Swaledale and Arkengarthdale.

Leave Reeth by the B6270 Richmond road and at the east end of the village, cross Reeth Bridge over the Arkle Beck. The bridge was built by John Carr in 1773. Pass Weighells Garage and yards along the road cross a stone wall stile with a double footpath sign on your left. Bear right, cross the stone stile and over the well used pasture path, go through another gated stile. The path turns right and continues uphill beside the wall on your right. Emerge out onto a lane above the hamlet of High Fremington and walk straight on for a short distance, then turn left up a narrow walled lane (barn on your left) for stiff climb up to another lane.

Turn left along this surfaced lane which was once the old miners' track to Hurst. Ignore the signposted bridleway BW Arkendale 4 miles on your left and steadily climb northwards up the main track, with unfolding views of Reeth wedged between Swaledale and Arkengarthdale. Pass the access to the white washed White House, where the bridleway deteriorates into an unenclosed stony track, which winds its way up the scarred limestone escarpment of Fremington Edge (1,250ft). At the top, before you go through the boundary gate, rest and enjoy one of the best viewpoints in Swaledale.

Once through the gate, there is a shorter route by turning left, westwards along Fremington Edge Top by the wall for two miles to Fell End. For the main route, walk straight on northwards and follow the old miners' track for a mile over Marrick Moor, giving distant views to the Cleveland Hills. As you approach Hurst the track drops down through a wilderness of spoil heaps and passes by one of two impressive chimneys. Go through a gate into the tiny hamlet of Hurst, once a thriving lead mining community. Turn left, pass Hall Farm and go through a couple of gates (last one marked Dogs Must Be On A Lead) and veer right up the broad track over the open moor, noting the redundant reservoir of Hurst Dam.

Head westwards up through the lead mining landscapes for a slow slog, especially with head on winds. Keep on the main track and just before a grouse butt marked No 1, turn left by a large spoil heap and follow the faint path which becomes a track up over the moor. Aim right through an open gap by a large stone gatepost in the corner ruined wall. Bear half left down the watery pasture towards Fell End with its twin cairns and before you reach this lofty spot curve right by a small cairn to the top of Fell End Lead Mine which closed in 1883. The path goes fairly steeply down through the old mine spoil heaps and although not too difficult a descent, great care should be taken when you scramble down the wet and slippery rocks.

At the bottom, pass a large spoil heap on your left and wind your way through the piles of stones to go down a delightful ridge path with views over Slei Gill to the hillside hamlet of Booze — a sober place with no pub. When you reach the bridleway signpost marked "Langthwaite" turn left through a metal gate and go downhill by the wall, with blue waymarkers, to come out by Storthwaite Hall — half house, half ruin.

Pass in front of this working farm, walk forward along the track and cross a railed footbridge over Slei Gill. Go up the gated concrete track to a double bridleway sign and turn left through a black gate and follow the track by the wood that takes you down to the Arkle Beck. At the metal footbridge, you can extend the walk by following the beckside track to Langthwaite for refreshments at the cosy Red Lion Inn, featured in All Creatures Great And Small and A Woman of Substance. For the return, a three mile meadowland route, cross the footbridge, turn left and immediately cross the stile on your left and negotiate Fore Gill Beck which might be difficult in flood. Continue along the beckside path and turn right through a concealed stile in the wall. Turn left along the field and follow the stiled field marked with yellow waymarks. The route is easy to follow, but constantly check the map and look out for a red painted footpath signpost that directs you along two fields further on, by the fenced farm of West Raw Croft with no access. Keep to the path through a series of waymarked stiles for another 1½ miles to curve right and come out by Sleights Brow on the Reeth Langthwaite road. Turn left for a road return back into Reeth.

10. Leyburn

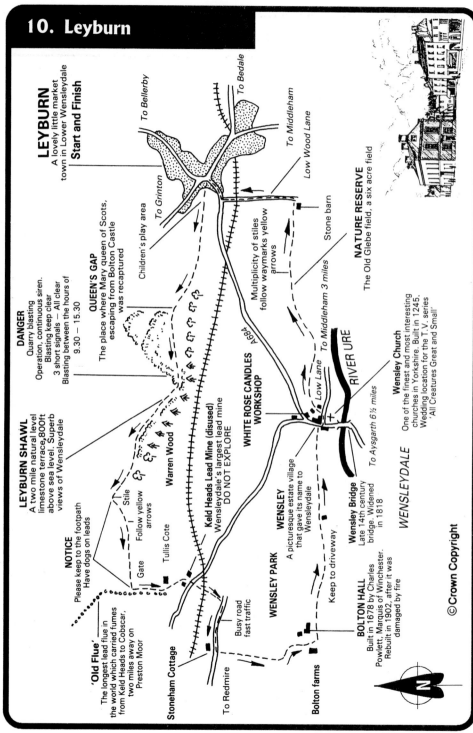

LEYBURN
A lovely little market town in Lower Wensleydale
Start and Finish

To Bellerby

To Bedale

To Grinton

To Middleham

Low Wood Lane

DANGER
Quarry blasting
Operation, continuous siren.
Blasting keep clear
3 short signals — All clear
Blasting between the hours of
9.30 – 15.30

QUEEN'S GAP
The place where Mary queen of Scots, escaping from Bolton Castle was recaptured

Children's play area

Multiplicity of stiles follow waymarks yellow arrows

Stone barn

NATURE RESERVE
The Old Glebe field, a six acre field

To Middleham 3 miles

LEYBURN SHAWL
A two mile natural level limestone terrace, 800ft above sea level. Superb views of Wensleydale

NOTICE
Please keep to the footpath
Have dogs on leads

Stile

Follow yellow arrows

Gate

Tullis Cote

Warren Wood

Keld Heads Lead Mine (disused)
Wensleydale's largest lead mine
DO NOT EXPLORE

WHITE ROSE CANDLES WORKSHOP

A684

Low Lane

RIVER URE

Wensley Church
One of the finest and most interesting churches in Yorkshire. Built in 1245.
Wedding location for the T.V. series
'All Creatures Great and Small'

'Old Flue'
The longest lead flue in the world which carried fumes from Keld Heads to Cobscar, two miles away on Preston Moor

WENSLEY
A picturesque estate village that gave its name to Wensleydale

WENSLEY PARK

Wensley Bridge
Late 14th century bridge. Widened in 1818

To Aysgarth 6½ miles

WENSLEYDALE

Stoneham Cottage

Busy road fast traffic

Keep to driveway

BOLTON HALL
Built in 1678 by Charles Powlett, Marquis of Winchester. Rebuilt in 1902, after it was damaged by fire

To Redmire

Bolton farms

N

42

10. Leyburn

Route: *Leyburn — Leyburn Shawl — Bolton Hall — Wensley — Leyburn.*
Distance: *Over 6 miles (10km). Easy field paths. Allow 4 hours.*
O.S. Maps: *Landranger Sheets 98, 99. Outdoor Leisure 30.*
Public Transport: *United Services 26 and 178. Richmond — Leyburn.*
Parking: *Market Place, Leyburn. Leyburn car park, off Market Place.*
Refreshments: *Hotels, cafes and pubs in Leyburn. The Three Horse Shoes, Wensley.*
Note: *Market Day is held on a Friday in Leyburn. Please keep to the footpaths and have dogs on leads. Keep to the driveway through Wensley Park. Do not explore Keldheads Lead Mine — the walls are unsafe and dangerous.*

This popular Leyburn loop provides a fine introduction to Wensleydale with extensive views. It follows the part of the Yoredale Way along the famous Leyburn Shawl including the Queen's Gap and returns through the unspoilt parkland of Bolton Hall to Wensley, the village that gave its name to Wensleydale.

Leave Leyburn Market Place by Commercial Square signposted "Way To The Shawl" and as directed, walk up Shawl Terrace. At the top, turn left, go through the kissing gate and follow the paved path on to Leyburn Shawl with superb views of Wensleydale including Penhill, as featured in James Herriot's Yorkshire.

Leyburn Shawl, a two-mile natural limestone terrace (800ft), is an attractive local walk laid out in 1841 and popular with generations of walkers. It is designated a permanent open space and owned by Lord Bolton. The path along The Shawl is obvious with directions unnecessary, but care should be taken near the escarpment edge with deep drops. Continue westwards along the stiled pastures and escarpment for a mile to reach the unsignposted Queen's Gap, where Mary Queen of Scots was recaptured after escaping from Bolton Castle. This historic spot is located opposite the high wire fence protecting the quarry on your right and before you cross the walled bridge with the old quarry tramway below. There are excellent views across Wensleydale to the beacon-crowned Penhill overlooking West Witton and Wensley with the castles of Middleham and Bolton, both visible.

As you progress along the wooded escarpment there is large notice warning you about the blasting operations at Leyburn Quarry, so don't be alarmed. At the end of Leyburn Shawl, straddle the waymarked wooden stile and go diagonally downhill to a tree with a notice — "Please keep to the footpaths and Have Dogs on Leads" — pass a waymarked upright boulder and proceed through the ruined wall. Continue diagonally down the pasture to cross a stile by a fallen tree and turn half right over the next field to go through the waymarked gate. Proceed westwards along the field following the waymark arrows to reach Keldheads Lane with similar signs about keeping to the paths and dogs on leads. Turn left through the blue metal gate with three waymark arrows and head down the unsurfaced lane. If you look over the wall on your right, you will see the collapsed Old Flue — the longest in the world which once carried fumes from Wensleydale's largest lead mine, Keld Heads or Keleds as it was called locally, to Cobscar, two miles away on Preston Moor.

Pass Tullis Cote Farm on your left and walk down the lane to pass Keld Heads Lead Mine with its tall square chimney connected to the ruined pump house. Cross the minor road, take the signposted path diagonally over the field and cross the Wensleydale Railway which still serves the Redmire Quarries. Cross a final field and exit through a gate to come out on to the Wensley-Castle Bolton road, where you leave the Yoredale Way. Turn right along the busy unclassified road for 880 yards and opposite Stoneham Cottage, turn down the lane (footpath signposted) with superb views up and down Wensleydale. Follow it all the way, turning left and right downhill passing the Bolton Farms on your right. At the bottom, turn left and pass Bolton Hall (private), home of the present Lord Bolton. The Hall was built in 1678 by Charles Powlett, Marquis of Winchester and, rebuilt in 1902, after serious fire damage.

Keep to the driveway for a mile through Wensley Park which brings you out into Wensley, the picturesque estate village that gives its name to Wensleydale.

If you require refreshments then The Three Horse Shoes is an excellent pub that welcomes walkers. Just above the pub, visit the White Rose Candles Workshop in Wensley Mill and see candlemakers Mick and Jen White at work and where all kinds of dipped and cast candles are made and sold on the premises.

Go down to Wensley Church, one of the finest and most interesting churches in Yorkshire. Built in 1245 with the tower added in 1719, it contains beautiful carved stalls, medieval brasses and wall paintings. The church was used as the wedding location in the TV series All Creatures Great And Small. From the church, walk along the minor road called Low Lane (signposted Middleham 3 - A6108) and after crossing the bridge over Wensley Brook, turn left uphill by Glebe Cottage for 160 yards and by some new houses, turn right through a waymarked wooden gate. From here

(Continued on page 44)

43

(Continued from page 43)

the Ō.S. map should be consulted frequently because of the multiplicity of stiles on the field path return. Head eastwards and follow the waymarks — yellow arrows — for the next 1½ miles across the narrow stiled pastures including a six-acre Nature Reserve named Leyburn Old Glebe Field. When you reach Low Wood Lane by a stone barn, turn left up this enclosed lane and return via the A684 back to Leyburn.

11. Askrigg

Route: *Askrigg — Worton Bridge — Woodhall — Carperby — Disher Force — Newbiggin — Askrigg.*
Distance: *Over 9 miles (14.5km) Allow 4/5 hours. Moderate.*
O.S. Maps: *Landranger Sheet 98; Outdoor Leisure Sheet 30.*
Parking: *On the cobbled area outside St. Oswald's Church, Market Place, Askrigg.*
Public Transport: *United Service 159. Leyburn — Hawes. Infrequent services, check timetables.*
Refreshments: *King's Arms Hotel; Crown Inn, Askrigg; The Wheatsheaf, Carperby.*

This popular ramble around Askrigg in the heart of Herriot Country is a classic for extensive views of Wensleydale.

Leave Askrigg by Cringley Lane, signposted F.P. Aysgarth/Worton Bridge, opposite the market cross and pass by the well known 'Skeldale House', the exterior television home and surgery, seen in the popular TV series of All Creatures Great and Small. Follow the lane which bends right and where it turns left, turn sharp right through an unsignposted squeeze stile by a gate on your right. Go down the field to the Wensleydale Railway for a short walk eastwards along the old railway track. Go through a rusty kissing gate and follow the flagged path south eastwards, diagonally across the stiled fields with fine views of Upper Wensleydale. Do not cross Worton Bridge, but turn left along the road and where it bends, cross a signposted stile on your right for a downstream riverside ramble via two footbridges to Nappa Mill.

Go up the farm road to a triple footpath sign by the stone bridge at the end of Thwaite Holme Lane. Cross the stile, turn right along the field and over a corner stile to reach the old Wensleydale Railway line which is private property and unfortunately not a right of way, although at first you must use the track to cross a metal ladder stile in the facing fence. The right of way runs parallel on the north side of the railway embankment. Two hundred yards eastwards from the railway bridge and yards beyond a double footpath sign, cross a half hidden stile for a short walk along the railway track. Fork left down through a rusty kissing gate and bear half right up the stiled fields with good views across Wensleydale to Addlebrough and down the dale to Lady Hill and Penhill.

At West End Farm, turn up Low Lane into the scattered farming hamlet of Woodhall to reach the Askrigg-Carperby road, where you can shorten the walk by half with a stiff climb northwards up a rutted track to rejoin the main route, but you will need to check this on the O.S. map.

For the main route, turn right along the Carperby road for over 880 yards. It's busy in summer, so take care and watch out for the oncoming traffic, as there is a sharp bend on the way. At the sign "Parking Place", cross the step stones over Eller Beck and once over the stile, signposted "Carperby", bear right, noting the lead mine spoil

St Oswald's Church, Askrigg

heaps below the wooded Haw Bank. Climb the sloping path up through the hazel wood and follow the field path eastwards through a succession of stiles. There is one stile with a high step which you might find difficult to straddle. The view across the valley reveals Bishopdale and Walden dominated by Penhill, plus the villages of Aysgarth and Thornton Rust. At Carperby football field turn left and right round this enclosed area and exit through a small gate with a nearby notice "Private — No Footpath Beyond This Point". Turn right down the track to the road. Go through the delightful Carperby village, boasting a 17th century market cross. At the far end of the village is The Wheatsheaf, where James Herriot and his wife, Helen, spent their honeymoon in 1941. The public bar offers bar meals, tea and coffee.

Beyond the village hall, turn left and go up the walled Hargill Lane, giving views of Bolton Castle. Where the lane splits, turn left through a red metal gate and follow the broad bridleway westwards, which climbs up to Carperby Stone Mine, famous for its huge flagstones. Keep on the green track which leads to another red gate marked "Farm Boundary — Please Keep Gate Closed". You have now reached the Ox Close Road, an old highway used by Lady Anne Clifford on her travels between Bolton Castle and Pendragon Castle. Follow the track westwards past Wet Groves lead

(Continued on page 47)

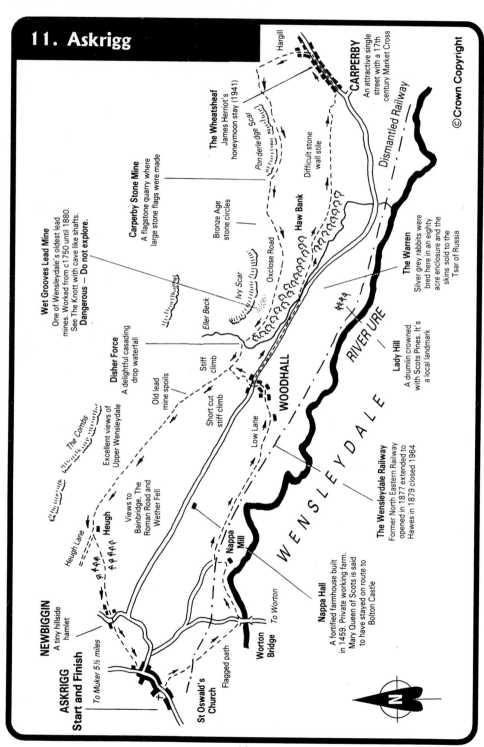

© Crown Copyright

CARPERBY
An attractive single street with a 17th century Market Cross

Hargill

The Wheatsheaf
James Herriot's honeymoon stay (1941)

Ponderledge Scar

Carperby Stone Mine
A flagstone quarry where large stone flags were made

Difficult stone wall stile

Bronze Age stone circles

Haw Bank

Oxclose Road

Wet Grooves Lead Mine
One of Wensleydale's oldest lead mines. Worked from c1750 until 1880. See The Knott with cave like shafts. **Dangerous — Do not explore.**

Ivy Scar

Eller Beck

The Warren
Silver grey rabbits were bred here in an eighty acre enclosure and the skins sold to the Tsar of Russia

Disher Force
A delightful casading drop waterfall

Stiff climb

Old lead mine spoils

Short cut stiff climb

WOODHALL

RIVER URE

Lady Hill
A drumlin crowned with Scots Pines. It's a local landmark

The Combs

Excellent views of Upper Wensleydale

Views to Bainbridge, The Roman Road and Wether Fell

Low Lane

WENSLEYDALE

Heugh Lane

Heugh

The Wensleydale Railway
Former North Eastern Railway opened in 1877 extended to Hawes in 1879 closed 1964

Dismantled Railway

NEWBIGGIN
A tiny hillside hamlet

Nappa Mill

Nappa Hall
A fortified farmhouse built in 1459. Private working farm. Mary Queen of Scots is said to have stayed on route to Bolton Castle

ASKRIGG
Start and Finish

To Muker 5½ miles

Flagged path

Worton Bridge

To Worton

St Oswald's Church

N

46

(Continued from page 45)

mine with its scattered spoil heaps below Ivy Scar. Once through a gate, ford the Eller Beck and note the delightful Disher Force which tumbles down the rocky outcrops.

Turn left and follow the gated track which turns left through a black metal gate overlooking Woodhall where both routes join. In yards, turn right up a stony track for a stiff climb and at the top, go through a wooden gate. Continue steadily upwards and westwards by the old lead mine spoil heaps with much of the walk above the 1,000ft contour. This high level route is the best part of the circuit and easy to follow through the upland pastures, which are waymarked and signposted for well over a mile. It offers extensive views of Upper Wensleydale, including Askrigg, Bainbridge, plus the Roman Road and the tops of Yorburgh and Wether Fell.

You come out above the isolated house called The Heugh and turn right along the walled Heugh Lane for a short walk and cross the unsignposted stone wall stile on your left. Go diagonally down a couple of stiled fields into a small wood, where, at the bottom, follow the waymarked stiled pastures south westwards down into the lovely little hamlet of Newbiggin. Pass Tofts Farm and walk into the walled lane by a large stone barn marked Horrabank. At the second stone barn, turn left through a squeeze stile by a gate and follow the waymarked stiled fields south westwards gradually downhill for a splendid return to Askrigg.

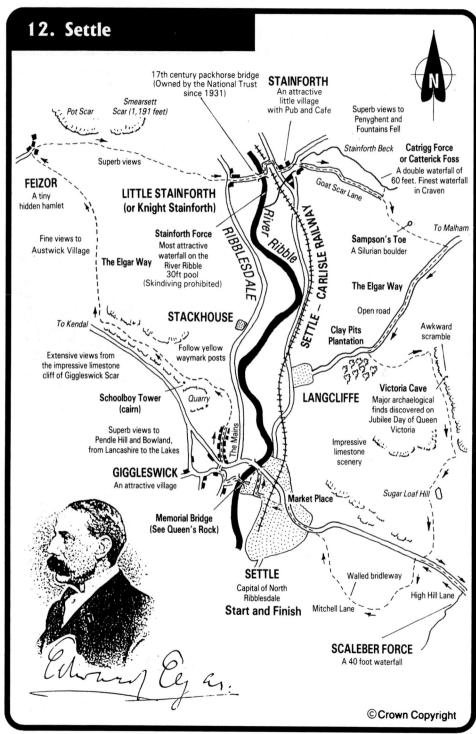

17th century packhorse bridge
(Owned by the National Trust
since 1931)

Pot Scar

Smearsett
Scar (1,191 feet)

STAINFORTH
An attractive
little village
with Pub and Cafe

Superb views to
Penyghent and
Fountains Fell

Stainforth Beck

**Catrigg Force
or Catterick Foss**
A double waterfall of
60 feet. Finest waterfall
in Craven

Superb views

Goat Scar Lane

FEIZOR
A tiny
hidden hamlet

**LITTLE STAINFORTH
(or Knight Stainforth)**

Fine views to
Austwick Village

The Elgar Way

Stainforth Force
Most attractive
waterfall on the
River Ribble
30ft pool
(Skindiving prohibited)

River Ribble

RIBBLESDALE

SETTLE — CARLISLE RAILWAY

To Malham

Sampson's Toe
A Silurian boulder

The Elgar Way

Open road

STACKHOUSE

To Kendal

Follow yellow
waymark posts

**Clay Pits
Plantation**

Awkward
scramble

Extensive views from
the impressive limestone
cliff of Giggleswick Scar

**Schoolboy Tower
(cairn)**

Quarry

LANGCLIFFE

Victoria Cave
Major archaelogical
finds discovered on
Jubilee Day of Queen
Victoria

Superb views to
Pendle Hill and Bowland,
from Lancashire to the Lakes

The Mains

Impressive
limestone
scenery

GIGGLESWICK
An attractive village

Sugar Loaf Hill

**Memorial Bridge
(See Queen's Rock)**

Market Place

Walled bridleway

SETTLE
Capital of North
Ribblesdale

Start and Finish

Mitchell Lane

High Hill Lane

SCALEBER FORCE
A 40 foot waterfall

12. Settle and the Elgar Way

Route: *Settle — Giggleswick — Giggleswick Scar — Feizor — Stainforth — Cattrigg Force — Victoria Cave — Sugar Loaf Hill — Scaleber Force — Mitchell Lane — Settle.*
Distance: *Over 13 miles (21km). Moderate with some stiff climbs. Allow 7 hours. Exposed in bad weather.*
O.S. Maps: *Landranger Sheet 98, Outdoor Leisure Sheets 2 and 10.*
Parking: *Ample parking in Settle. Use the Market Place, Settle.*
Refreshments: *Pubs, cafes, hotels in Settle; cafe and Craven Heifer in Stainforth.*
Note: *The publication "Elgar in the Yorkshire Dales" can be obtained from Mr W.R. Mitchell, Castleberg, 18 Yealands Avenue, Giggleswick, Settle, North Yorkshire, price £2.70 with postage. A leaflet on The Elgar Way, price 20p from above address plus SAE or from Tourist Information Centre, Town Hall, Settle, North Yorkshire.*

The Elgar Way, a new walk in North Ribblesdale, is a 13-mile long loop devised by Bill Mitchell, retired editor of the Dalesman and named after Edward Elgar, the famous composer, linking his excursions with his close friend Dr Charles William Buck, through the limestone landscapes of Yorkshire.

Leave Settle Market Place via Bishopdale Court, left of the cafe called Ye Olde Naked Man (the name amused Elgar), turn right along Kirkgate and pass Victoria Hall where Dr Buck used to conduct the local orchestra. Next to the hall, the large house was Dr Buck's birthplace. Go under the railway viaduct and follow Kirkgate into Church Street (A65) and before Settle Bridge, turn left by Ribble Terrace and along the riverside park to Kings Mill.

Turn right, keep between the white painted lines and cross Giggleswick Memorial Bridge (erected 1982) over the River Ribble noting the great rock called Queen's Rock. Turn left and bear half right up the tarmac path through a ginnel into the attractive village of Giggleswick. Turn right along Bankwell Road, and pass Rose Cottage, the home of the late Russell Harty.

Turn right up Belle Hill and see Cravendale, Dr Buck's home, where Elgar was a frequent visitor. Cross the busy A65 and turn left up The Mains, where at the end of the cul-de-sac, an unsurfaced track, cross a ladder stile and bear right diagonally up a rough stony path for a stiff climb. This rough route is punctuated by yellow painted posts.

Hug the fenced path alongside a large limestone quarry and follow the yellow waymarks to a double footpath signpost which directs you northwards along the impressive Giggleswick Scar for a mile. Admire the panorama across Craven Country into Lancashire and to the Lakes, from Pendle Hill to Bowland and beyond. No wonder it was one of Elgar's favourite walks.

After crossing a second high ladder stile, bear half right across the pleasant pastures and look out for a short waymarked post that points the way through a signposted handgate (Giggleswick 1½ miles). Bear half right, cross two more ladder stiles, pass a bridleway signpost and go down a rutted track into the tiny hidden hamlet of Feizor. Turn

Stainforth's packhorse bridge

right and beyond the bungalow, leave Feizor by a stile, signposted Stainforth 1½ miles.

Go up a sunken way (packhorse route) by a wall for a gradual climb over the stiled walls and continue up a greentrack through a shallow pass with the craggy outcrops of Pot Scar and Smearsett Scar way up to your left. At the top of the ridge, look down on the Ribble Valley with Pennine panorama of Penyghent and Fountains Fell. Go down a winding track into Little Stainforth, known locally as Knight Stainforth. Cross the road, pass the 17th century Stainforth Hall and at the bottom of the lane is Stainforth Bridge, a 17th century packhorse bridge, owned by the National Trust since 1931. This was a favourite spot for Elgar.

If you want to see Stainforth Force, one of the most attractive waterfalls on the River Ribble, cross the stile on your right before the bridge and follow the rocky riverside to the waterfall with a 30 foot pool (skin diving prohibited). Return, cross the bridge over the River Ribble and follow the lane up to a bridge over the Settle-Carlisle Railway to reach the B6479. Turn right, cross the road and take either road into the attractive little village of Stainforth which boasts a shop/cafe and pub called the Craven Heifer.

Leave Stainforth for a steep climb of 880 yards up Goat Scar Lane and at the top cross the ladder

(Continued on page 50)

49

(Continued from page 49)

stile on your left for a downhill walk (slippery) to Catrigg Force, the finest waterfall in Craven Country. This double waterfall of 60 feet was another favourite haunt of Elgar. Return to the lane and take the ladder stile adjacent to the gate and turn right up the sloping pasture with extensive Pennine panorama. Cross a stile, signposted "Winskill ½ mile" and bear half right, then veer left along a narrow walled enclosure. Cross another stile and veer right to join an open surface farm road that takes you past a Silurian boulder called Sampson's Toe.

At the T-junction (Langcliffe/Cowside road) turn right along the road for a mile until it descends and turn left up a gated car track by Clay Pits Plantation and follow this past a barn and once through a metal gate, turn immediately right and cross a ladder stile, signposted "Stockdale Lane 1½ miles".

Follow the stony path by the wall with Langcliffe Scar above. If you want to see Victoria Cave, scramble up the rocky scree path on your left and see this remarkable archaeological site discovered in 1837 which yielded ancient animal life and early human presence. It's the highest point on the Elgar Way.

Return with care down the steep scree slope back to the main route. Follow the path by the wall, cross a ladder stile and continue down the stony path with impressive limestone outcrops all round. Below Attermire Scar, turn right through a waymarked open gap in the wall, pass the ruined rifle range and turn left over a stile with a triple signpost and follow the uphill path to the right of Sugar Loaf Hill and continue along the field to exit over a corner stile into Stockdale Lane.

Turn right along this lane and left along High Hill Lane for 880 yards to see Scaleber Force, a 40ft waterfall in a wooded ravine, another waterfall frequently visited by Elgar and Buck. Retrace your steps and use the signposted Mitchell Lane which joins the old coach route back to Settle to complete the Elgar Way.

Trails of the riverbank — the Wear from Bishop Auckland.

Wandering along the Waggonway from Wylam.

Hundale Point off the Cleveland Way from Scarborough.

Roseberry Topping lies ahead on the walk from Great Ayton.

13. Hawes

Route: *Hawes — Hardraw — Cotterdale — High Dike — Cotter End — Mossdale Head — Appersett — Hawes.*
Distance: *14 miles. Strenuous. Allow 8 hours.*
O.S. Maps: *Landranger Sheet 98; Pathfinder 608 (NY80/SD89).*
Parking: *National Park Centre fee car park, Hawes. Two free car parks in Hawes.*
Public Transport: *United: Service 26, Richmond to Hawes. Check timetables.*
Refreshments: *Plenty of pubs, cafes and hotels in Hawes. The Green Dragon Inn; Coach House Cafe; The Carthouse Tearoom, Hardraw.*
Note: *Do not attempt in doubtful weather, dangerous in mist. Use map and compass.*

This long loop is one of the best hill walks in the Yorkshire Dales, and if not, in all England.

Leave Hawes by the Brunt Acres Road opposite the children's play area and head north in the direction of Hardraw. At the entrance of Hawes Rural Workshops, cross the signposted stile and follow the Pennine Way diagonally along the flagstone paths through two fields to rejoin the same road. Turn left along the road, cross the twin arched Haylands Bridge over the River Ure and follow the road for a further 150 metres (see the sign) northwards. When the road climbs above the tree line, turn left, cross the stepped stile (signposted Hardraw/Pennine Way) and westwards, follow the paved pastures through nine squeeze stiles, over the former Wensleydale golf course, with a request to keep in single file, all the way to Hardraw — and an invitation to see Hardraw Force, the highest unbroken waterfall in Britain (further details in walk 14).

From Hardraw, turn left, cross the bridge and beyond the old school (dated 1875), a guidepost "Pennine Way — B.W. Cotterdale 4; Thwaite 8", directs you right up the walled lane — it's the old coal road to the pits of Hearne and Cotterdale. Dog owners should heed the warning — "Please keep dogs on a lead — Dogs chasing sheep will be shot". Follow the Pennine Way for a mile and plod up the old miners' track. At the end of the walled lane, cross a high ladder stile and emerge onto the open fell. Start going up again for a slow slog, with excellent views across Hearne Beck to the Buttertubs overshadowed by Lovely Seat (2,213ft). A mile further on, as the green track winds above Hearne Top, cross a further high ladder stile and take your last look down Wensleydale. At the bridleway signpost, you leave the Pennine Way which traverses northwards for Great Shunner Fell on the distant horizon.

As directed, ("B.W.Cotterdale") turn left for a mile along the high level gated track passing below the tall Humesett Beacon, with splendid views down into the isolated little valley of Cotterdale. Stride out along by the shake holes and look out for an unsignposted gate with a notice "Do not start fire" to enter South Wood, part of the extensive Cotterdale Forest. If you miss this gate entrance, you'll end up at Cotterdale Coal Pits, where coal was mined by candlelight. Descend

the track curving left, then right and left again, down a broad forest drive. As you descend, look out for a path on your right (you can easily miss it), and at the bottom of the wood, go over a stile and cross the footbridge over East Gill. Follow the track and enter the tiny hamlet of Cotterdale with two farms and ten cottages. Pass Shepherds Cottage (dated 1616) and the renovated cottage called The Old Chapel (private house) was the local chapel which last buried its dead some 25 years ago. On one of the upright gravestones in the garden are said to be the words "We repose in peace" dedicated to some unknown soul. A local is said to have given the obvious reply — "We all ken who they are, and when we're all gone, what'll it matter anyway". Years ago, a rhyme related to the three principal families who lived in this dead end dale, whose names were Hall, Kirk and King:

Three Halls, two Kirks and a King,
Same road out as goes in

Walk through this peaceful place and just before a crude cottage with a bellcote above its doorway, there is a signposted stile on your right. You might experience some difficulty crossing this because of some sheep feeder troughs on the other side, so use the nearby gate. Walk straight on, pass the barn buildings and follow the path through the gated fields alongside West Gill and in the third field, cross a stile with care, where the fence and wall meet.

Cross over West Gill (it might be difficult after heavy rain) and once over another stile, bear right and ascend the path into Cotterdale Forest. Brace yourself for the start of a pull out of the valley for a mile up the steep slope grass path between the forest of sitka spruce. Cross over a stony forest drive and continue straight on upwards, where the real hard work starts and as you climb, bear a thought for the pall bearers and mourners who followed this burial route to the tiny church of Lunds. You are following Cotterdale's Corpse Way.

At the top of the wood, you've earned your rest and look back into Cotterdale. Over a stile, head westwards up the pathless moor (check map) with some more climbing. Look out for a couple of

(Continued on page 57)

13. Hawes

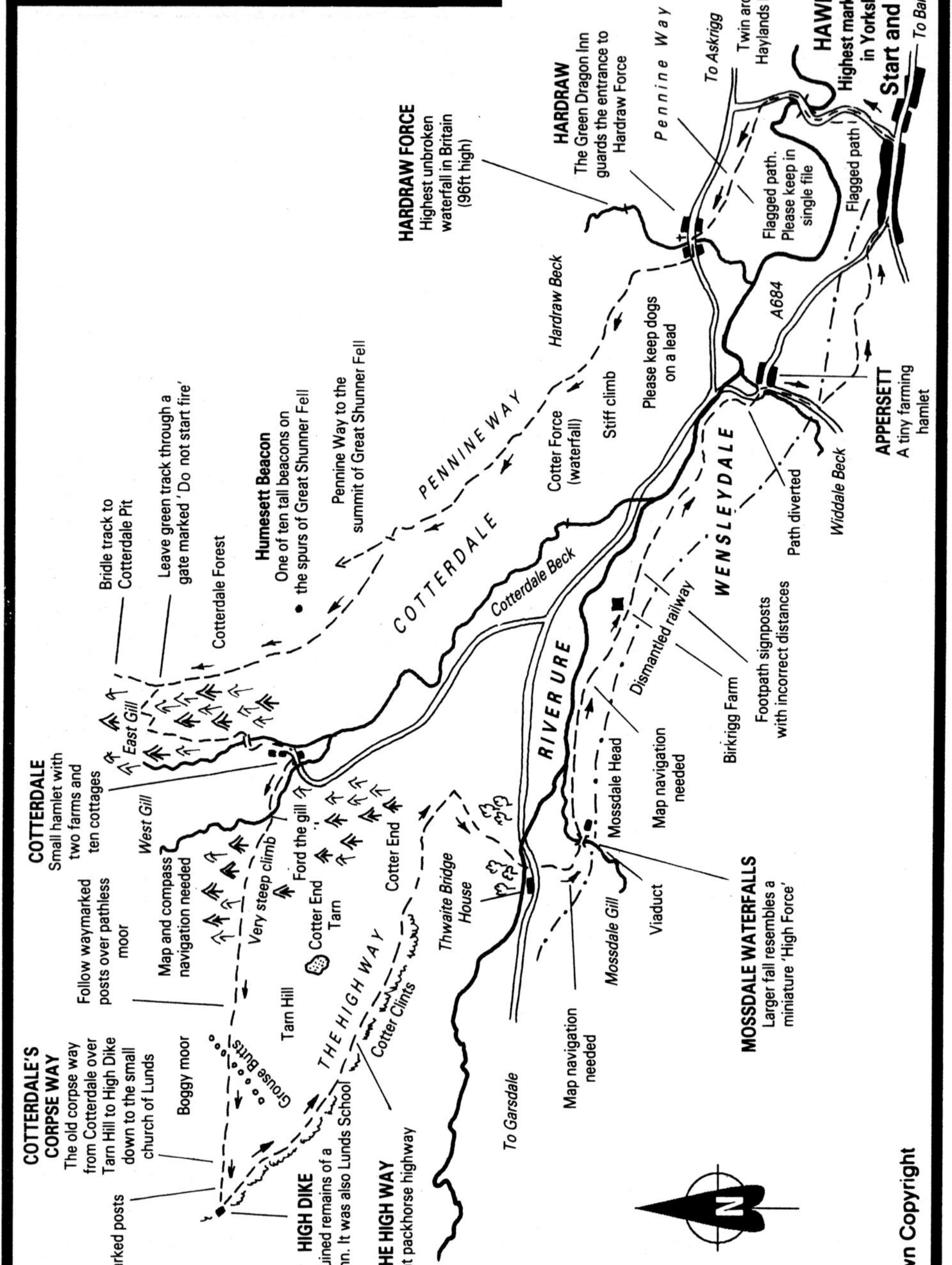

HAWES
Highest market town in Yorkshire.
Start and Finish

To Bainbridge

Twin arched
Haylands Bridge

To Askrigg

HARDRAW
The Green Dragon Inn
guards the entrance to
Hardraw Force

Pennine Way

Flagged path.
Please keep in
single file

Flagged path

HARDRAW FORCE
Highest unbroken
waterfall in Britain
(96ft high)

Hardraw Beck

A684

Please keep dogs
on a lead

Stiff climb

APPERSETT
A tiny farming
hamlet

Bridle track to
Cotterdale Pit

Leave green track through a
gate marked 'Do not start fire'

Cotterdale Forest

Humesett Beacon
One of ten tall beacons on
the spurs of Great Shunner Fell

Pennine Way to the
summit of Great Shunner Fell

Cotter Force
(waterfall)

PENNINE WAY

COTTERDALE

Cotterdale Beck

Widdale Beck

Path diverted

WENSLEYDALE

RIVER URE

COTTERDALE
Small hamlet with
two farms and
ten cottages

Follow waymarked
posts over pathless
moor

Map and compass
navigation needed

West Gill

East Gill

Ford the gill

Very steep climb

Cotter End
Tarn

Cotter End

Tarn Hill

THE HIGH WAY

Cotter Clints

*Thwaite Bridge
House*

Dismantled railway

Birkrigg Farm

Footpath signposts
with incorrect distances

Map navigation
needed

Mossdale Head

Viaduct

Mossdale Gill

**COTTERDALE'S
CORPSE WAY**
The old corpse way
from Cotterdale over
Tarn Hill to High Dike
down to the small
church of Lunds

Waymarked posts

Boggy moor

Grouse Butts

HIGH DIKE
Ruined remains of a
packhorse inn. It was also Lunds School

THE HIGH WAY
Ancient packhorse highway

To Garsdale

Map navigation
needed

MOSSDALE WATERFALLS
Larger fall resembles a
miniature 'High Force'

N

© Crown Copyright

(Continued from page 55)

posts (faintly waymarked) and aim for the horizon to reach a corner railed fence. Pass through a line of grouse butts and head westwards down the moor on a good path for another mile, following the line of waymarked posts. Watch out and detour round a very boggy section.

When you see the ruined High Dike Farm, you will find some of the best views in Britain before you, including Mallerstang, Wild Boar Fell and Whernside. Facing the ruined High Dike Farm — once a popular inn for packmen until 1877 and which housed Lunds School — turn left, eastwards and stride out along this old pack horse route called the High Way for an airy upland walk with splendid views.

Hug the wall along the rutted track and admire the extensive views over the valley, including the engineering marvel of the Dandy Mire Viaduct carrying the Settle-Carlisle Railway. The track dips down, crosses Johnston Gill and after 880 yards, passes some deep shake holes (natural holes) and climbs uphill. The path levels out along the limestone terrace above Cotter Clints (1500ft) with some glorious walking and superb views. It's hard to imagine that this old road was used by the Queen of the North, Lady Anne Clifford, when she visited her castles at Appleby, Brough and Pendragon in the mid-17th century.

After two miles, the hillside spur of Cotter End is reached with panoramic views of Upper Wensleydale and Cotterdale. The track winds down below an old lime kiln and aim through the narrow gate left of another gate. Descend the hillside and halfway down, you have a choice of two stiles, cross either over the wall and bear half right down the rough pasture and aim for the far side of a narrow woodland. Cross the ladder stile, head diagonally down the pathless pasture and look for a hidden stile giving access into the woodland below.

Go down the wood to come out by Thwaite Bridge House. Cross Thwaite Bridge over the River Ure and on the other side of the A684, cross the signposted stile for an uphill walk. Keep by the wall, check map and once over the brow of the hill, branch half right and aim for a newly-erected stile in the bottom corner of the pathless field.

Cross the stile, turn left through an open gateway (yellow waymarks) for a short walk down into the secluded Mossdale, a picturesque place with lovely waterfalls.

Cross the farm bridge over Mossdale Gill and the upper falls, situated below the four-arched Mossdale Viaduct, painted by Britain's greatest artist, J.M.Turner (1775-1851). Through the gateway, a bench seat has been provided by the Wensleydale Tourist Association for those places associated with Turner as part of The Turner Trail.

As you approach Mossdale Head Farm, turn left between the waymarked barn buildings and pass behind the farm. Follow the yellow waymarks and aim half left through a waymarked gate. Keep by Mossdale Gill which becomes the River Ure and continue straight on, but check the map as you leave the river and come to a securely tied rusty gate with an adjacent railed fence. In the next field, follow the path by an electric fence to reach a double footpath which directs you left along a gated farm road. Follow this for a mile to pass Birkrigg Farm and reach a triple signpost with confusing mileages.

Leave the farm road and continue straight on following the footpath signs through the valley bottom fields for an unexpected climb up the wooded hillside, high above the River Ure. Turn left and follow the stiled (signposted) pastures eastwards for another mile to rejoin the River Ure for a riverside ramble to New Bridge. Here you can follow the diverted path or road walk into the tiny farming hamlet of Appersett. Once over the bridge, turn immediately right and climb up the narrow lane with views of the delightful waterfalls on Widdale Beck.

Go under Appersett Viaduct and turn left through a gate with a notice stating that there is no right of way along the old railway line. Turn half right up the first field with excellent views of Wensleydale and cross a ladder stile. Aim half left over the next field and in front of a gate (do not go through), turn left along the field edge and cross a stone stile at the far end of the field. Turn half left, aim for a open wall gap and go down a rutted muddy track to come out onto the A684 near the Ashes. A short walk up the road brings you back to Hawes.

© Crown Copyright

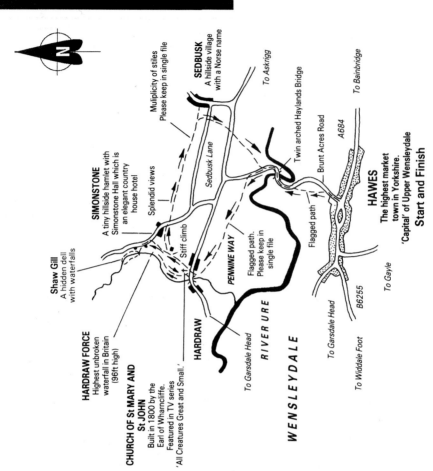

N

SEDBUSK
A hillside village with a Norse name

Muliplicity of stiles
Please keep in single file

To Askrigg

Sedbusk Lane

Twin arched Haylands Bridge

To Bainbridge

A684

Brunt Acres Road

SIMONSTONE
A tiny hillside hamlet with Simonstone Hall which is an elegant country house hotel

Splendid views

Flagged path.
Please keep in single file

PENNINE WAY

Flagged path

Stiff climb

HAWES
The highest market town in Yorkshire.
'Capital' of Upper Wensleydale
Start and Finish

Shaw Gill
A hidden dell with waterfalls

HARDRAW

To Gayle

B6255

To Garsdale Head

RIVER URE

To Garsdale Head

To Widdale Foot

HARDRAW FORCE
Highest unbroken waterfall in Britain
(96ft high)

CHURCH OF St MARY AND St JOHN
Built in 1800 by the Earl of Wharncliffe.
Featured in TV series 'All Creatures Great and Small.'

WENSLEYDALE

58

14. Hawes

Route: *Hawes — Hardraw — Simonstone — Sedbusk — Hawes.*
Distance: *Under 5 miles. Easy. Allow 2/3 hours. All field walk with one stiff climb.*
O.S. Maps: *Landranger Sheet 98, Outdoor Leisure 30, Hawes Footpath Map, Stile Publications.*
Parking: *National Park Centre car park, Hawes. Fee. Two free car parks in Hawes.*
Public Transport: *United Services. Richmond to Hawes. Check timetables.*
Refreshments: *Plenty of pubs, cafes and hotels in Hawes. The Green Dragon Inn, Coach House Cafe, The Carthouse Tea Room, Hardraw.*
Note: *Waterfall entrance through the Green Dragon Inn only. Admission fees: Adults 40p, children 20p, senior citizens 20p, children under five years free. Dogs must be kept on leads at all times. Please keep in single file.*

This amble is a real favourite with my family in autumn and whenever we are in Yorkshire's highest market town of Hawes in Upper Wensleydale we cannot resist a visit to see Hardraw Force, the highest unbroken waterfall in Britain.

Leave Hawes by the Brunt Acres Road, opposite the children's play area and head north in the direction of Hardraw. At the entrance of Hawes Rural Workshops, cross the signposted stile and follow the Pennine Way diagonally along the flagstone paths through two fields to rejoin the same road. Turn left along the road, cross the twin arched Haylands Bridge over the River Ure and follow the road for a further 150 metres (see the sign) northwards. When the road climbs above the tree line, turn left, cross the stepped stile, (signposted ''Hardraw/Pennine Way'') and westwards, follow the paved pastures through nine squeeze stiles, over the former Wensleydale golf course, with a request to keep in single file, all the way to Hardraw.

Enter the tiny village of Hardraw by the Coach House Cafe, opposite The Green Dragon Inn which guards the entrance to Hardraw Force. The only access to the waterfall is through the pub, so pay your admission and follow the path on either side of the Fossdale Beck to see Wensleydale's spectacular attraction: Hardraw Force — the highest unbroken waterfall in Britain. Its white water plummets over a 96ft drop, a perfect sight after heavy rain. You are requested not to go behind the waterfall. Remember your safety is your own responsibility.

Return to the Inn for refreshments or try the cafe or tea room. Outside the Inn, turn left, pass the apartments' entrance and go through the backyard of the end cottage on your right. Follow the flagged path signposted to Simonstone, uphill by the wall on your left for a stiff climb. At the top,

cross the stepped stile and admire the wonderful backward views of Upper Wensleydale, including Yorburgh (1,686ft) and Wether Fell (2,015ft).

Climb again, where a notice states that dogs must be kept on leads at all times. Turn right through a squeeze stile and pass in front of West House Farm. Here you have a choice of routes. Either cross the flagged path diagonally in single file to the hillside hamlet of Simonstone with its elegant Simonstone Hall or go up the farm track to the road and turn left for a short walk to the signposted Shaw Gill Wood and explore the delightful Shaw Gill, a hidden dell with waterfalls and paved paths. Return along the same road, pass Simonstone Hall and at the east end of this tiny hamlet, cross the stile on your left (signposted ''Sedbusk'') for a level walk eastwards with extensive views. Although the path is easy to follow, the only demanding part of the walk is negotiating a succession of squeeze stiles (17 in all, including two high ladder stiles) with a request to keep in single file.

As you approach the little village of Sedbusk, check the map and two fields away, bear half right down the field and cross the bottom corner stile into Sedbusk Lane, with wonderful views of Wensleydale. Turn right along the lane for a few yards and cross the stone wall stile on your left, signposted ''Haylings Bridge''. Go down the meadow, pass by a barn and aim upwards over a high stone wall stile. Proceed diagonally over the crest of the hill and down to another stile and out onto the Askrigg road. Turn right along this for a few yards and cross the stile on your left (signposted ''Haylings Bridge ½ mile'') for a final field finish over a lovely long, pleasant pasture via an isolated packhorse bridge to reach the Brunt Acres Road. Follow the outward route back to Hawes to complete my favourite family walk.

15. Bainbridge

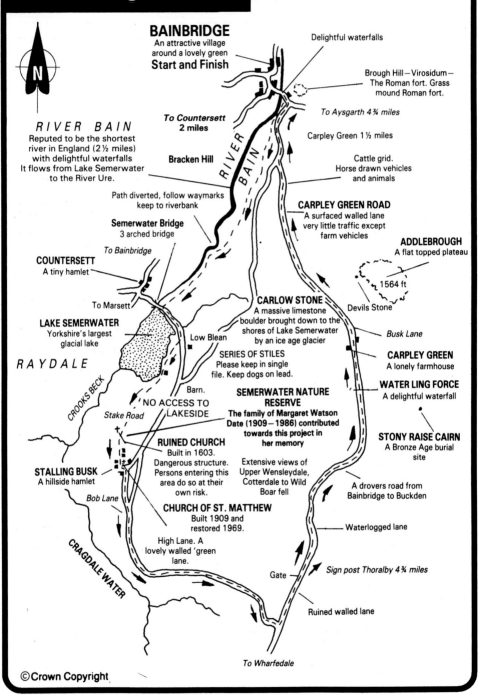

BAINBRIDGE
An attractive village around a lovely green
Start and Finish

Delightful waterfalls

Brough Hill — Virosidum — The Roman fort. Grass mound Roman fort.

To Countersett 2 miles

To Aysgarth 4¾ miles

Carpley Green 1½ miles

Bracken Hill

R I V E R   B A I N
Reputed to be the shortest river in England (2½ miles) with delightful waterfalls It flows from Lake Semerwater to the River Ure.

Cattle grid. Horse drawn vehicles and animals

RIVER BAIN

Path diverted, follow waymarks keep to riverbank

CARPLEY GREEN ROAD
A surfaced walled lane very little traffic except farm vehicles

Semerwater Bridge
3 arched bridge

ADDLEBROUGH
A flat topped plateau

To Bainbridge

COUNTERSETT
A tiny hamlet

1564 ft

To Marsett

CARLOW STONE
A massive limestone boulder brought down to the shores of Lake Semerwater by an ice age glacier

Devils Stone

LAKE SEMERWATER
Yorkshire's largest glacial lake

Low Blean

Busk Lane

R A Y D A L E

CARPLEY GREEN
A lonely farmhouse

SERIES OF STILES
Please keep in single file. Keep dogs on lead.

WATER LING FORCE
A delightful waterfall

CROOKS BECK

Barn.
NO ACCESS TO LAKESIDE

SEMERWATER NATURE RESERVE
The family of Margaret Watson Date (1909 – 1986) contributed towards this project in her memory

STONY RAISE CAIRN
A Bronze Age burial site

Stake Road

RUINED CHURCH
Built in 1603. Dangerous structure. Persons entering this area do so at their own risk.

Extensive views of Upper Wensleydale, Cotterdale to Wild Boar fell

A drovers road from Bainbridge to Buckden

STALLING BUSK
A hillside hamlet

CHURCH OF ST. MATTHEW
Built 1909 and restored 1969.

Waterlogged lane

Bob Lane

High Lane. A lovely walled 'green lane.

Gate

Sign post Thoralby 4¾ miles

CRAGDALE WATER

Ruined walled lane

To Wharfedale

15. Bainbridge

Route: *Bainbridge — Lake Semerwater — Stalling Busk — High Lane — Busk Lane — Carpley Green — Bainbridge.*
Distance: *9 miles (14.5km). Moderate. Allow 4½ to 5 hours. Easy to follow. Field paths and walled lanes.*
O.S. Maps: *Landranger Sheet 98, Outdoor Leisure Sheet 30.*
Parking: *Limited roadside parking in Bainbridge. No parking on The Green.*
Public Transport: *United Services 26 Richmond to Hawes.*
Refreshments: *Rose and Crown Hotel, Bainbridge. None on route.*

Anyone who loves the winding green ways of the Yorkshire Dales will certainly enjoy this walk which is one of the best from Bainbridge in Upper Wensleydale. It combines popular paths with ancient highways and links the shortest river in England with the legendary Lake Semerwater. Leave Bainbridge by the A684 Aysgarth road and over the river bridge, note the picturesque stepped waterfalls. Before the Stalling Busk road, turn right through the stile, signposted "Semerwater 2 miles". In yards, fork left up the footpath signposted hillside of Out Brough and follow the path with the wall yards away to your left. The path dips down by a walled enclosure (double footpath sign) with a barn building and ascends Bracken Hill (1,100ft), where there are excellent views into Raydale with your first sight of Semerwater and backward views to Askrigg. On top of this small summit there are a couple of stiles, take the signposted one on the right and at the bottom of the hill follow the path through the waymarked stiled fields. When you cross a high ladder stile by a rusty gate, turn immediately right, as the path has been diverted and follow the waymarks to the river bank. You have now reached the River Bain, 2½ miles long and reputed to be the shortest river in England.

Follow the stiled riverside path southwards to come out by Semer Water Bridge. Walk to the foreshore of Lake Semerwater, Yorkshire's largest glacial lake steeped in local legend. The most famous relates to a drowned town beneath its waters, sunk by a poor man's curses after he was refused food and drink. Those immortal words are:

Semer Water rise! Semer Water sink!
And swallow all save this lile house
that gave me food and drink.

The Carlow Stone is a massive limestone boulder brought down by an ice age glacier to the lakeland shore. Legend has it that the Carlow Stone was hurled by a giant from Addlebrough at his Satanic Majesty on Crag Hill. The stone that the devil returned fell short of its target and can be seen 200 feet below the summit of Addlebrough. It is called the Devil's Stone. Another story states that the Carlow Stone attracts local couples who are about to marry because it is lucky to touch the stone for prosperity and many children.

Turn left along the lakeland lane for 880 yards to Low Blean Farm and opposite turn right over the high ladder stile, signposted "Stalling Busk 1 Mile". From the stile, walk along the pleasant pastures (muddy) through a series of stiles (three in all with yellow waymarks) and admire the surrounding views with Addlebrough (1,564ft) behind you. Pass a barn on your left and the signposted route leads you down a muddy stiled path, very close to the lake with no access to the shore. Beyond the lake cross two stiles to enter the new Semerwater Nature Reserve.

The family of Margaret Watson Dale (1909-1986) contributed towards this project in her memory. Steadily climb up the rough pastures on a good path (signposted) through three gated stiles to reach the ruined church of Stalling Busk (900ft) with access via a slit stile. The old church was built in 1603, rebuilt in 1722 on the same site and abandoned in 1909. The churchyard has excellent views of Raydale and Semerwater. From the church, turn right and immediately bear half left through the ruined wall and look out for the signpost "Stalling Busk" which directs you uphill for 880 yards with a 200 foot stiff climb above the wooded beckside to the hillside hamlet of Stalling Busk. Turn right, then left and call in at the beautiful tiny Church of St Matthew built in 1909.

Outside the church, pass Home Farm and turn left by Bells Cottage to ascend Butts Lane and halfway up this surfaced lane, turn right up the walled Bob Lane for rutted ascent to High Lane. Turn right along this level walled lane with good views down into the bracken covered Cragdale. Stride out along this lovely green track, one of the best old highways in the dales, for about two miles, giving extensive views over Wensleydale to Wild Boar Fell. The lane twists and turns to reach Busk Lane coming in from your left. For an easy return route, with detailed direction not needed, turn left into this ruined walled lane and follow it northwards, downhill for some superb views of Addlebrough. After two miles, pass the farm of Carpley Green and follow the surfaced Carpley Green Road (traffic free), giving lovely views of Lake Semerwater and see if you can spot the Devil's Stone on the shoulder of Addlebrough. It's a straightforward downhill walk of two miles back into Bainbridge.

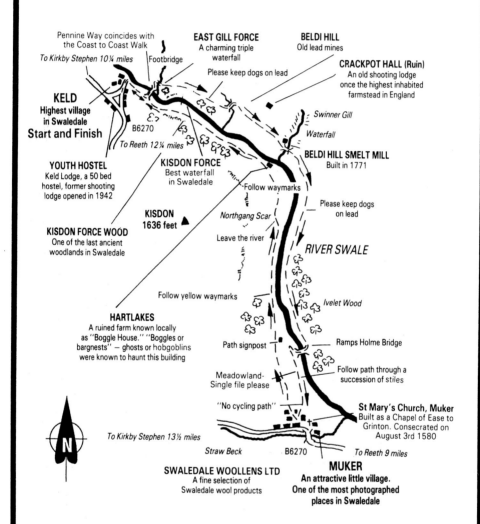

Pennine Way coincides with the Coast to Coast Walk

To Kirkby Stephen 10¼ miles Footbridge

EAST GILL FORCE
A charming triple waterfall

Please keep dogs on lead

BELDI HILL
Old lead mines

CRACKPOT HALL (Ruin)
An old shooting lodge once the highest inhabited farmstead in England

KELD
Highest village in Swaledale
Start and Finish

B6270

To Reeth 12¼ miles

Swinner Gill

Waterfall

BELDI HILL SMELT MILL
Built in 1771

YOUTH HOSTEL
Keld Lodge, a 50 bed hostel, former shooting lodge opened in 1942

KISDON FORCE
Best waterfall in Swaledale

-Follow waymarks

Please keep dogs on lead

KISDON
1636 feet ▲

Northgang Scar

Leave the river

RIVER SWALE

KISDON FORCE WOOD
One of the last ancient woodlands in Swaledale

Follow yellow waymarks

Ivelet Wood

HARTLAKES
A ruined farm known locally as "Boggle House." "Boggles or bargnests" — ghosts or hobgoblins were known to haunt this building

Path signpost

Ramps Holme Bridge

Meadowland-Single file please

Follow path through a succession of stiles

"No cycling path"

St Mary's Church, Muker
Built as a Chapel of Ease to Grinton. Consecrated on August 3rd 1580

N

To Kirkby Stephen 13½ miles

Straw Beck   B6270   *To Reeth 9 miles*

SWALEDALE WOOLLENS LTD
A fine selection of Swaledale wool products

MUKER
An attractive little village.
One of the most photographed places in Swaledale

16. Keld

Route: Keld — Swinner Gill — Ramps Holme Bridge — Muker — Kisdon Force Wood — Keld.

Distance: Under 6 miles (10km). Fairly easy. Allow 3/4 hours.

O.S. Maps: Landranger Sheet 98. Outdoor Leisure 30. Upper Swaledale Footpath Map Stile Publications.

Parking: Limited roadside parking in Keld. Do not obstruct gateways.

Public Transport: United Service 30 Richmond to Keld. Check timetables.

Refreshments: None in Keld. The Farmers Arms — leave rucksacks outside — Muker Tea Shop; Old School Tea Room; The Old Vicarage Licensed Restaurant in Muker.

Note: This walk can equally start from Muker. Meadowland single file please.

If you want to show visitors the most spectacular and beautiful walk in Upper Swaledale, take them on this easy to follow, popular walk between Keld and Muker, on both sides of the river, within a stone's throw of the Swale. Leave Keld by Keld Lane at the bottom of the village, signposted "Public Footpath To Muker" and follow the Pennine Way east for 440 yards. At the two-way Pennine Way sign, turn down the stony wooded hillside path; pass through a gate and cross the wooden footbridge (rebuilt in 1951) over the River Swale. Go up the path to the track above with the triple waterfall of East Gill Force away to your right. Here the Coast to Coast Walk intersects the Pennine Way. Leave the latter and follow Alfred Wainwright's Coast to Coast Walk eastwards along the track, over the bridge above the falls and through a gate. Keep on the track through two gates with signs requesting "Please Keep Dogs On A Lead" and "Please Close The Gate".

Go up the stony track and along by the flanks of Beldi Hill, with stunning Swaledale views back to Keld and Great Shunner Fell (2,340ft), highest point in Swaledale. From this high level path, pause and admire the views across the wooded Kisdon Gorge to Kisdon Hill (1,636ft) with Kisdon Force below, but not seen. The track curves over a tiny stone arch bridge and look back to see the spoil heaps of the Beldi Lead Mine, a reminder of Swaledale's bygone lead mining industry. Stay on the main track by the wall and you leave the Coast to Coast Walk which forks left for the ruined Crackpot Hall. Go downhill by East Wood for a stiff descent where the track winds down through a gate to the bottom of the impressive Swinner Gill with superb views down the valley to Muker. Cross the railed footbridge by the ruined Beldi Smelt Mill built in 1771. There is a splendid waterfall tucked in behind these lead mine remains. Walk southwards for 1½ miles, slanting down a stony stretch of track (hard on the feet) for a pleasant stroll along the banks of the river. This is the best part of the walk on short cropped grass. The path becomes a track again and when it swings left uphill, walk straight on and cross Ramps Holme Bridge over the River Swale. Turn right along the railed riverside signposted "Muker" and left through a

squeeze stile with a sign "Meadowland Single File" Please. Follow the easy field path route through a series of squeeze stiles across the meadows and pass Stoneleigh on your right, as you enter the attractive village of Muker with its pub, tea rooms, shops, post office and tiny church. The Swaledale Woollens shop is well worth a visit.

For the return, leave Muker by the same route, except pass to the left of Stoneleigh and follow the Kisdon Road past the Old Vicarage and just beyond the bungalow called Breconside, where the unsurfaced road branches left for Kisdon, walk straight on and go through the unsignposted, small metal corner gate with a tiny sign "Please Shut Gate". Follow the enclosed path northwards and after the third gate, a slanting green path leads down to a barn with a footpath signpost "Keld". Continue straight on, northwards above the fenced riverside, through at least four stiles with yellow waymarks. Exit through a small wooden gate on your right to the riverside path. Walk upstream, noting the valley views and after 880 yards (check map) veer half left and aim for a waymarked stile by the ruined wall patched with wooden rails.

Now follow the waymarks northwards through a succession of stiled fields, noting the ruined farm of Hartlakes, a field away to your right. It's known locally as "Boggle House" where Boggles or Barguests ghosts or hobgoblins were known to haunt this disused farmstead. The route climbs up between a sunken low walled path, giving good views of the ruined remains of the Beldi (low level) lead mine across the valley. Go through a gate into Kisdon Force Wood, one of the last ancient woodlands in Swaledale. It's a steady uphill climb on a stony track through the limestone cliffs of Kisdon Gorge called White Waller. At the two way footpath sign you have joined the Pennine Way and follow this well worn path westwards. Further on, the footpath sign Kisdon Force gives you the opportunity to view Swaledale's best double waterfalls, but it is a scramble down with a stiff return and stout footwear is definitely needed. Follow the Pennine Way back to Keld to complete this splendid riverside circuit.

© Crown Copyright

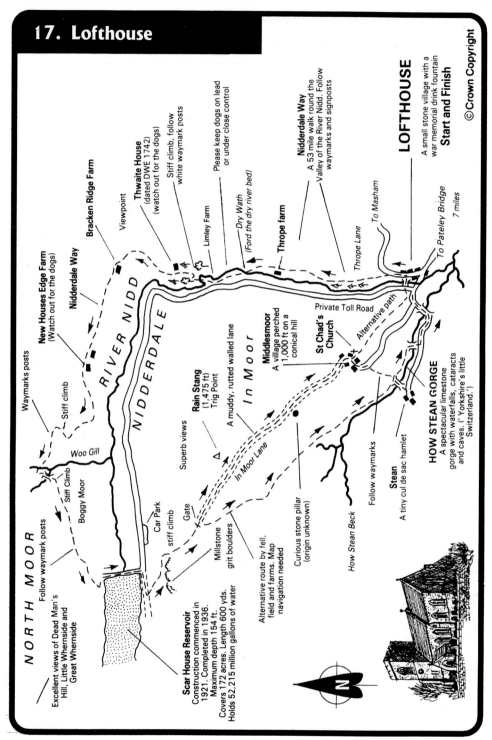

LOFTHOUSE
A small stone village with a war memorial drink fountain
Start and Finish

To Masham

To Pateley Bridge
7 miles

Nidderdale Way
A 53 mile walk round the Valley of the River Nidd. Follow waymarks and signposts

Thrope Lane

Thrope farm

Dry Wath
(Ford the dry river bed)

Limley Farm

Please keep dogs on lead or under close control

Stiff climb, follow white waymark posts

Thwaite House
(dated DWE 1742)
(watch out for the dogs)

Viewpoint

Bracken Ridge Farm

New Houses Edge Farm
(Watch out for the dogs)

Nidderdale Way

Waymarks posts

Stiff climb

Stiff Climb

Woo Gill

Boggy Moor

Private Toll Road

Alternative path

St Chad's Church

Middlesmoor
A village perched 1,000 ft on a conical hill

Rain Stang
(1,475 ft)
Trig Point

A muddy, rutted walled lane

In Moor

Superb views

In Moor Lane

Curious stone pillar
(origin unknown)

HOW STEAN GORGE
A spectacular limestone gorge with waterfalls, cataracts and caves. (' Yorkshire's little Switzerland.')

Stean
A tiny cul de sac hamlet

Follow waymarks

How Stean Beck

Car Park
stiff climb

Gate

Millstone grit boulders

Alternative route by fell, field and farms. Map navigation needed

Scar House Reservoir
Construction commenced in 1921. Completed in 1936. Maximum depth 154 ft. Covers 172 acres. Length 600 yds. Holds 52,215 million gallons of water.

NORTH MOOR
Follow waymark posts

Excellent views of Dead Man's Hill, Little Whernside and Great Whernside

RIVER NIDD

NIDDERDALE

N

17. Lofthouse

Route: *Lofthouse — Limley Farm — Bracken Ridge — Woo Gill — Scar House Reservoir — Middlesmoor — How Stean Gorge — Lofthouse.*
Distance: *Over 10 miles (16km). Allow 5½ hours including visit to How Stean Gorge. Moderate. Easy to follow.*
O.S. Maps: *Landranger Sheet, 99 Pathfinder Sheet SE 07/17, Outdoor Leisure 30.*
Parking: *Village car park, Lofthouse.*
Refreshments: *Crown Hotel, Lofthouse. Crown Hotel, Middlesmoor. How Stean Cafe.*
Note: *A fine, clear day with good visibility is essential.*

See Nidderdale in a nutshell and try one of the best upland walks in this forgotten valley of the Yorkshire Dales. It uses part of the Nidderdale Way and offers superb views.

Leave Lofthouse by walking up the village, past the war memorial drink fountain with quaint verses. Pass the Post Office, climb up the road and where it bends right, turn left along the level track signposted "Nidderdale Way". Go through a gate and follow the track called Thrope Lane through the gated fields for a mile. There are fine views on both sides of the valley. Continue northwards down past the haunted Thrope House into a walled lane with waymarks to reach Dry Wath where the River Nidd has gone underground. Cross the dry river bed and aim right for the largest ladder stile you have ever seen. Cross this and follow the waymarked path (yellow arrows) by the wire fence and turn right over another ladder stile, then left upstream. Cross a stile, turn right, follow the waymarks through a gate (signposted "Nidderdale Way") and proceed along the farm track with a request to "Please keep dogs on lead or close control", to reach Limley Farm. Waymarks direct you behind the farm and then left by the barn and down through some rough vegetation to ford the dry river bed.

Go through a small gate, follow the path by the moss covered-wall and as you approach a stone barn (check the map) turn right up the bridle track for a steep climb up the bracken hillside. If you miss this turn-off, there is an alternative route further on where white waymarked posts ascend the same hillside for a steady climb. At the top both paths join and lead into a short walled lane and through a gate. Watch out for the dogs. Turn left and left again by Thwaite House (dated DWE 1742) and right behind the farm into a walled lane and out into open country. Stride out along this high level track with excellent views of Nidderdale. Keep on this gated track which contours round to Bracken Ridge. Just before the farm, turn right and then left, westwards to pass above the farm with Scar House Reservoir seen on the skyline. Continue on this level track to pass New Houses Edge and watch out for the dogs. Go down over a beck with a small waterfall and when you reach a Nidderdale Way, sign turn right and ascend the gated track. It winds left and then swings sharp right for a stiff climb and forks left up through

a gate to North Moor. Proceed westwards over the moor and follow the white waymarked posts along a rough track that dips down over Twizling Gill and drops unexpectedly into a deep ravine called Woo Gill. Ascend the well-made track, go acutely right and follow the track through a gate.

Follow the waymarked posts over the open soggy moor, where the path keeps by the wall and exits through a gate. Walk straight on and the bridle track swings left via the walkers shelter down to Scar House Reservoir. Cross the dam head with crenellated turrets and at the far side a couple of plaques tell you that the first sod was cut on October 5, 1921 with work completed on September 7, 1936. Marvel at this man-made construction set in a bleak wilderness surrounded by Dead Man's Hill, Little Whernside and Great Whernside. From the dam, turn right along the water board road and at the double Nidderdale Way signpost turn left up the stony track which zigzags between the millstone grit boulders for a stiff climb. At the top admire the views and proceed through a gate into In Moor Lane. The direct route is straight down the rutted walled lane although, as shown on my map, there is an alternative route for the more ambitious walker which leaves the lane through an unsignposted gate on your right for a field/farm walk down into the How Stean Valley.

For the easy walk, go down the lane (very muddy) for two miles into Middlesmoor, a tiny village perched on a conical hill about 1,000 feet above sea level. The church of St Chad is well worth a visit. There is an excellent walk down to Lofthouse from this lofty spot. From Middlesmoor walk down the road and opposite a barn turn right through a stile signposted "Public Footpath Stean" and follow the stiled path to a bridge over How Stean Beck. This is Nidderdale's main attraction, How Stean Gorge, a spectacular limestone gorge with caves and waterfalls. It's a miniature Grand Canyon and classed as Yorkshire's "Little Switzerland". Backtrack and follow the gated field path southwards to How Stean Cafe and pay your admission to see the 70 feet dramatic ravine. For the last leg of the walk, follow the Lofthouse road to the layby and take the signposted field path, which crosses the toll road and the River Nidd to complete a classic circuit back in Lofthouse.

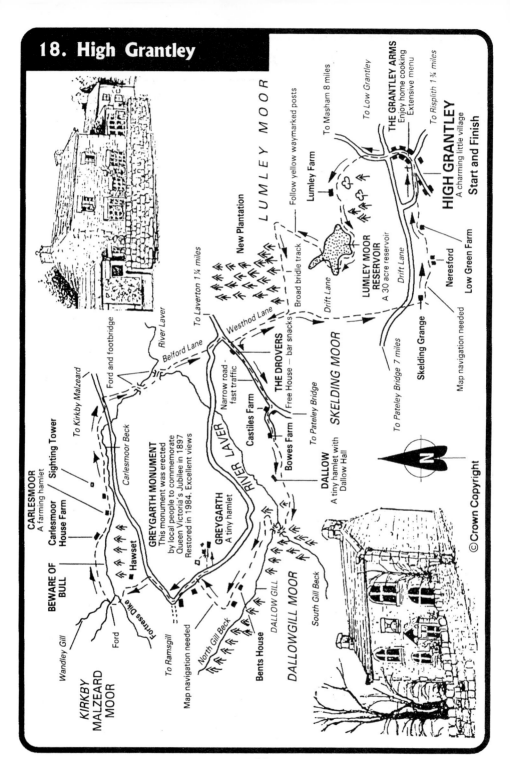

KIRKBY MALZEARD MOOR

Wandley Gill

Ford

Fortress Dike

To Ramsgill

BEWARE OF BULL

Hawset

CARLESMOOR
A farming hamlet

Carlesmoor House Farm

Sighting Tower

To Kirkby Malzeard

Carlesmoor Beck

GREYGARTH MONUMENT
This monument was erected by local people to commemorate Queen Victoria's Jubilee in 1897. Restored in 1984. Excellent views

GREYGARTH
A tiny hamlet

Map navigation needed

North Gill Beck

DALLOW GILL

Bents House

DALLOWGILL MOOR

South Gill Beck

Ford and footbridge

River Laver

To Kirkby Malzeard

Belford Lane

To Laverton 1¼ miles

Narrow road - fast traffic

RIVER LAVER

Castiles Farm

Bowes Farm

DALLOW
A tiny hamlet with Dallow Hall

Westhod Lane

THE DROVERS
Free House — bar snacks

To Pateley Bridge

New Plantation

LUMLEY MOOR

Follow yellow waymarked posts

To Masham 8 miles

Lumley Farm

To Low Grantley

THE GRANTLEY ARMS
Enjoy home cooking
Extensive menu

To Risplith 1¾ miles

HIGH GRANTLEY
A charming little village

Start and Finish

Broad bridle track

Drift Lane

LUMLEY MOOR RESERVOIR
A 30 acre reservoir

SKELDING MOOR

Drift Lane

Skelding Grange

Map navigation needed

Neresford

Low Green Farm

To Pateley Bridge 7 miles

N

© Crown Copyright

18. High Grantley

Route: *High Grantley — Lumley Moor Reservoir — Dallow — Greygarth Monument — Carlesmoor — Belford Lane — Drift Lane — High Grantley.*
Distance: *13½ miles. Moderate. Allow 7 hours. Fields, moorland tracks, leafy lanes and some road walking.*
O.S. Maps: *Landranger Sheet 99, Pathfinder Sheets SE27/37; 630 (SE17/18); 653 (SE26/36).*
Parking: *Limited roadside parking at west end of High Grantley.*
Refreshments: *The Grantley Arms, High Grantley; The Drovers, Dallowgill.*
Note: *I wish to thank Alison Meek of Grange Cottage, High Grantley, for permission to use her line drawings of High Grantley.*

Discover Dallowgill, a delightful little dale — one of Yorkshire's best kept secrets — 2½ miles west of Kirkby Malzeard. It's off the beaten track and the perfect place for peace and solitude. Start this figure of eight walk from the charming village of High Grantley and walk up the Masham road for 880 yards. Go through the footpath signposted gate on your left, bear half right down the field and cross the stile into Ruddings Plantation. Follow the path down and up the wood to exit over a stile into a lane. Turn left along this to pass Lumley Farm and reach Lumley Moor Reservoir. Cross the top of the dam for a delightful walk round the reservoir and at the north east side cross a facing stone stile by the Scots Pine, giving access to Lumley Moor. Walk up to a waymarked post (3 yellow arrows) and follow the line of waymarked posts, north eastwards up the moor pasture and aim for a stone stile (difficult to spot), some 30 yards from the wall corner. Cross the stile, turn left along the gated bridleway by New Plantation and follow this for 880 yards to reach Westhod Lane. Turn up this lane (it's also the return route) for 880 yards to reach the Dallowgill road. Walk up the road and make sure you call in at The Drovers.

Continue for 880 yards and turn right into a walled lane with a "No Through Road" symbol by Castiles Farm and follow it downhill to pass Bowes Farm. The lane becomes a track as it dips down to Dallow, with Hall Farm and a row of renovated cottages. Exit through a gate and follow the lower track by the woodland. Pass through a gate and descend the larch lined track down into Dallowgill, a delightful woodland valley, where at the bottom cross a white painted footbridge over South Gill Beck. Go through the gate, turn right along the track and cross another white painted footbridge, this time over North Gill Beck. Climb out of the wood and at the top, beyond a gate on your left, look out for a stile behind the wall, also on your left. Cross this and there is another stile immediately on your left in the wall. Go diagonally down the field and pass through a gate to re-enter the woodland. Turn right keep to the path just within the top of the woodland edge, with views westwards over this secluded valley to Dallowgill Moor, Hambleton Hill (1,331ft) and on the skyline a white-washed shooting lodge can be seen. At the

end of the wood go through a gate and out into the open fields, with a wall on your left. Watch out for the flying pheasants as you progress westwards through the gated fields to pass by Bents House. Follow the same line of path through the fields to reach a couple of derelict barn buildings, where the route swings right up a little used gated farm track to the Dallowgill road. A short diversion can be made by turning right down the road to Greygarth Monument, a short stone tower that dominates the skyline of Dallowgill erected in 1897 to commemorate Queen Victoria's Jubilee and restored in 1984. Climb the ladder inside the monument and enjoy the extensive views across to the Vale of Mowbray and to the Cleveland Hills. Retrace your steps and follow the open moor road westwards for 880 yards to Tom Corner, where the Shooters Inn closed in 1932.

At the road signs, turn right along the Kirkby Malzeard road and to the north on the moor horizon you can see another tower called Carle Tower, which I understand was used as a lookout during Cromwell's days. After 440 yards follow the track northwards onto Carle Moor. It fords Wandley Gill and ascends the moor, where you turn right through a wedged wooden gate into a walled lane. Follow this delightful bridle track eastwards for over 1½ miles. This is a lovely walk, but watch out for the bull. As you approach the last farm, where track splits walk forward by the farm to see the stone built Sighting Tower which is linked by a tunnel from Leighton Reservoir.

Retrace your steps and take the lower track eastwards to rejoin the Kirkby Malzeard road. Turn up this and at the top, turn right down a leafy lane to cross a footbridge over Carlesmoor Beck and watch out for a very watery section before you reach another footbridge over the River Laver. Go up the ancient Belford Lane for a mile to reach the road near The Drovers.

Return by Westhod Lane (already walked) and head southwards for a mile down Drift Lane over Skelding Moor to reach the road. For an easy return road walk along Drift Lane back to High Grantley or alternatively use the field path route eastwards of Skelding Grange with map navigation needed to complete this satisfying excursion.

19. Grewelthorpe

© Crown Copyright

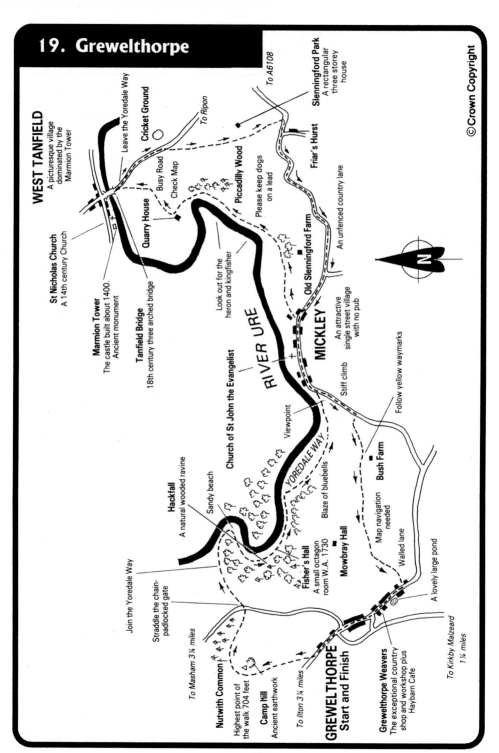

WEST TANFIELD
A picturesque village dominated by the Marmion Tower

Leave the Yoredale Way

Cricket Ground

To Ripon

Busy Road
Check Map

Quarry House

To A6108

Slenningford Park
A rectangular three storey house

Piccadilly Wood
Please keep dogs on a lead

Friar's Hurst

Old Slenningford Farm
An unfenced country lane

St Nicholas Church
A 14th century Church

Marmion Tower
The castle built about 1400. Ancient monument

Tanfield Bridge
18th century three arched bridge

Look out for the heron and kingfisher

RIVER URE

MICKLEY
An attractive single street village with no pub

Stiff climb

Follow yellow waymarks

Church of St John the Evangelist

Viewpoint

YOREDALE WAY

Bush Farm

Hackfall
A natural wooded ravine

Sandy beach

Blaze of bluebells

Map navigation needed

Fisher's Hall
A small octagon room W.A. 1730

Mowbray Hall

Walled lane

A lovely large pond

Join the Yoredale Way

Straddle the chain-padlocked gate

To Masham 3¾ miles

Nutwith Common
Highest point of the walk 704 feet

Camp Hill
Ancient earthwork

To Ilton 3¼ miles

GREWELTHORPE
Start and Finish

Grewelthorpe Weavers
The exceptional country shop and workshop plus Haybarn Cafe

To Kirkby Malzeard 1¼ miles

N

19. Grewelthorpe

Route: *Grewelthorpe — Camp Hill — Hackfall — Mickley — West Tanfield — Slenningford Park — Mickley — Grewelthorpe.*
Distance: *5 miles (8km) or about 10 miles (16km). Fairly easy to moderate. Allow 3 to 6 hours. Field, riverside and woodland paths. Some road walking.*
O.S. Maps: *Landranger Sheet 99, Pathfinder Sheet SE 27/37.*
Parking: *Limited roadside parking in Grewelthorpe. No official car park. Do not inconvenience residents.*
Refreshments: *Haybarn Cafe; Grewelthorpe Handweavers; The Crown Inn; The Hackfall Inn, Grewelthorpe. Bull Inn; Bruce Arms, West Tanfield.*

This two-in-one walk, a short loop within a large loop, explores the lesser known country around the pleasant straggling village of Grewelthorpe, three miles south of Masham. It's a splendid walk via pleasant pastures, through deep woods and follows part of the Yoredale Way along the banks of the River Ure linking the picturesque villages of Mickley with West Tanfield. There is some road walking on quiet country lanes. Both walks use the same outward and return routes.

Start the walk at the north end of Grewelthorpe village and take the road signposted "Ilton 3¼" and walk up Nutwith Lane. Beyond The Elms, look for a post with a footpath sign missing. It's on your right. Go through the waymarked squeeze stile and diagonally left up the waymarked stiled pastures, three in all, with unfolding views. Away to your right is a small hill with a trig point top called Horsepasture Hill with the ancient earthwork of Camp Hill. Turn right downhill by the hedge and follow the yellow arrows bearing left for a handgate (waymarked) into the larch woodland of Nutwith Common.

Do not go uphill, but turn right by the wall and follow the path round and down the woodland edge to the forest drive below. Turn right along this for a truly lovely walk — a carpet of bluebells in the right season. At the Thorpe Road turn left along this and in yards at the Public Footpath signpost, turn right through a metal gate if you can. It's chain padlocked so straddle the gate and go down the delightful gated pastures of Limehouse Hill into the woods of Hackfall where you encounter the Yoredale Way, a 100 mile walk from York to Kirkby Stephen. Go down the wood and follow the River Ure downstream. It's a well trodden route so expect plenty of mud even in dry weather. When you see a sandy beach the path swings away from the river and follows the undulating woodland for about 1½ miles eastwards. On the way you will pass the ruined Fisher's Hall, a small stone room. Beyond this spot pass some rocky outcrops and keep on the main path.

Do not be tempted to take one of the many paths out of the woods. There are a few yellow waymark arrows on the way. Leave the wood through a clearing planted with young trees and here high above the river enjoy the superb views of the weir below. Pass the sign "Riverside Path"

and join the road below High Bank. Rest a while at the seat before you decide on the long or short route back to Grewelthorpe. For the long loop turn left along the road to the single street village of Mickley. At the east end of the village turn left along the walled lane signposted "Footpath to Tanfield Only" with a request "Please Keep Dogs on a Lead". Cross the stile and follow the path across the field and aim between the strip woodland. Cross another stile and turn left along by the wood and field of growing crops. Over a further stile and through the bush scrubland follow a track eastwards to join a delightful riverside path. You may be lucky to see a kingfisher along the stretch of river.

Continue along the river by Piccadilly Wood and up the steep wooded slope, exit over a waymarked stile on your left into a pasture. Bear half right and check the map as there is no access into the next field so go along to the far right corner of the same field to two open gateways and out through a gate with Quarry House away to your left. Turn right along the farm road for 880 yards to reach Tanfield Bridge where you leave the Yoredale Way. Cross the bridge into West Tanfield, one of the most picturesque villages in Yorkshire. Tanfield Castle, built about 1400 and commonly called the Marmion Tower, is well worth a visit. There are two pubs in the village.

Leave Tanfield, recross the bridge and follow the busy A6108 road southwards for 880 yards where opposite the cricket ground at the sign "Public Footpath Friar's Hurst" turn left along the parkland path for 880 yards. Pass to the right of Slenningford Hall, an elegant rectangular, three-storey house, and follow the driveway out of the parkland. Note there is a right of way marked on the O.S. map that directs you right from the driveway by four trees through a securely tied gate and along the field edge with no sign of a path to come out through some scrubland with no access to the road opposite Friar's Hurst. Turn right along the unfenced country lane with very little traffic for a mile return to Mickley.

For the short loop go along the lane for another 880 yards (part walked on the outward route) and climb up the steep High Bank and follow this downhill until a public footpath sign on your right

(Continued on page 70)

(Continued from page 69)

directs you over a stile by a gate. Follow the path along the field and look out for the former field boundary where on your right a double waymarked post directs you diagonally up the field and aim through the wooden gate. Turn right through the open gateway, pass the pond and go up the edge of the hillside and cross the field corner stile. Bear half left for a concealed waymarked stile on your left in the hedgerow. Cross this and from here constantly check the map, preferably the Pathfinder Sheet, to traverse the waymarked stiled fields that lead you into an enclosed hedgerowed lane back to Grewelthorpe.

Views by the bucketful at Robin Hood's Bay.

The castle towers above the Swale at Richmond.

Gravestones of the Baker-Bakers — on the Sherburn stroll.

Stepping stones as you walk out from Wolsingham.

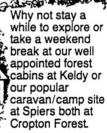

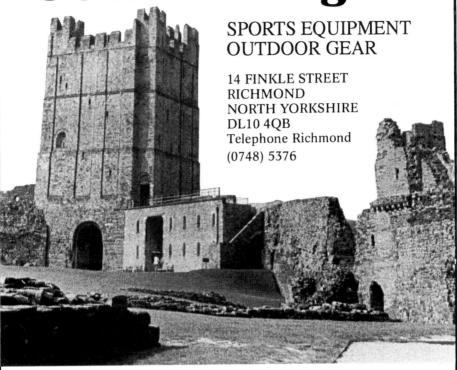

20. Wolsingham

Fishing
Opened in 1977 for public fishing. Well stocked with trout. Fishing is by fly only. Permit system operates

Tunstall House Farm

NATURE RESERVE
(No Entry)
N.R. created to protect sensitive marshland vegetation

Check map
Turn right

Backstone Bank Railway Depot
(ruined remains)

Stiff climb

Track of disused railway
(Waskerley — Tow Law Railway)

PICNIC AREA
Picnic tables, car park and toilets

Ancient oak woodland designated S.S.I.S.

Gate marked BEWARE BULLS

A Finnish log cabin fishing lodge

TUNSTALL RESERVOIR

Backstone Bank Farm

TUNSTALL RESERVOIR
Acreage 112
HT.a.o.d. 720ft
Constructed 1879

Tunstall Treatment Works

△ Triangulation
Point (1,159ft)

Heather clad moor
View point — extensive views over wild Weardale

Waskerley Beck

Quiet unclassified road
Expect farm and visitor traffic to reservoir

Old sand pits

*WOLSINGHAM
N O R T H   M O O R*

Rutted Track

Bishop oak

Thistlewood Farm

High Doctor Pasture

Baal Hill House

To Tow Law 3 miles

B6296

Warning
Deep Water

follow waymarks
(yellow arrows)

Beck

Thornhope

•WOLSINGHAM
An unspoilt little town in Lower Weardale
Start and Finish

Demesne
Mill Picnic
Area

Market Place

To Crook

To Stanhope

A689

R I V E R

Eastgate — Bishop Auckland Railway

W E A R

W E A R D A L E
(Valley of the Prince Bishops)

©Crown Copyright

20. Wolsingham

Route: Wolsingham — Bishop Oak — Tunstall Reservoir — Tunstall House — Backstone Bank Railway Depot — Wolsingham North Moor — Wolsingham.
Distance: About 8 miles (12.8km) Moderate with a steep climbs and includes unavoidable road walking. Allow 4 hours.
O.S. Maps: Landranger Sheets 92, 87, 88. Pathfinder First Series NZ03, NZ04.
Parking: Market Place, Wolsingham.
Public Transport: Weardale Motor Services service 101 Bishop Auckland—Wolsingham.
Refreshments: The Black Bull; The Beehive; Pegotty's Cafe; The Bay Horse Hotel in Wolsingham. None on route.
Note: Please keep dogs under strict control.

This popular field and fell walk explores the lovely Tunstall Valley, north of Wolsingham and includes extensive views over wild Weardale.

From Wolsingham Market Place follow the B6296 Lanchester road and just beyond St Anne's High School, turn left into Demesne Mill picnic area, a delightful spot by the Waskerley Beck. Stay by the beck and when you see the sign "Warning — Deep Water", aim for a kissing gate with a hidden waymarked post in the far left corner of the same field. Walk straight on over the long field to cross a short railed footbridge. Walk forward, cross a waymarked stile and turn right along the well-worn path to cross another waymarked stile. Cross the footbridge over Thornhope Beck, climb the steps and hug the fence on your right and head northwards for a rusty metal kissing gate with two waymark arrows. Do not walk straight on, but turn left and follow the hedgeside path steadily up the field to reach a second kissing gate with yellow circle marked "Public Footpath". Continue up the next field and exit through a final kissing gate (signposted Public Footpath) to reach the road directly opposite the entrance drive to Fawnlees Hall.

Turn right and follow the unclassified road northwards for 1½ miles to pass High Doctor Pasture and the ancient hunting lodge of Bishop Oak with its unique dovecote. A little further on, pass the Tunstall Treatment Works and a stiff climb up the road reveals the mile-long Tunstall Reservoir built in 1879 for the Weardale and Shildon Water Board. Pass the entrance to the dam head and follow the reservoir road for 600 yards to reach the car park/picnic area with its purpose built fishing lodge. Stay here awhile and admire the variety of trees, bird life and flowers in this lovely sheltered valley.

Leave the picnic area, turn right along the road to Tunstall House Farm where the road ends and turn down the very rough stony track. Pass the Nature Reserve (No Entry) created to protect the sensitive marshland vegetation and carry on over the stone bridge which spans the head of the reservoir. Go through the waymarked wooden gate marked "No Road For Cars — Private" and tackle the steep unsurfaced track for a climb up to 1,050 feet above sea level which is the last real climb on the walk.

As you near the ruined remains of the old Backstone Bank railway depot on the disused Tow Law—Waskerley railway, turn right (check map) and follow a track through a facing gate for the return route which is nearly all downhill. Head south down a couple of rough pastures with the wall away to your right and do not be deterred by the sign "Beware Bulls" marked on the second field gate. Unless I have been lucky, I have never ever encountered any bulls in these pastures. At the top, cross a stile and continue along the level pathless pasture, noting the excellent views of wild Weardale and the bleak moorland topped with television masts on Collier Law and Horse Shoe Hill.

After a mile of rough pasture walking, you reach the heather-clad Wolsingham North Moor which is very impressive in August with its purple heather. Keep southwards on a good path and pass to the right of the white triangulation point (1,159ft), the highest point on the walk. Pause and admire the impressive all round views.

The path becomes a track as it leaves the moor via a gate and heads down a rutted track past the disused sand pits on your right. Follow this gated track with views of Wolsingham and exit through a white gate to join a narrow farm lane. Pass the entrance to Thistlewood Farm and continue down this lane for under a mile to reach the B6296. Follow this road back to Wolsingham to complete a lovely afternoon amble.

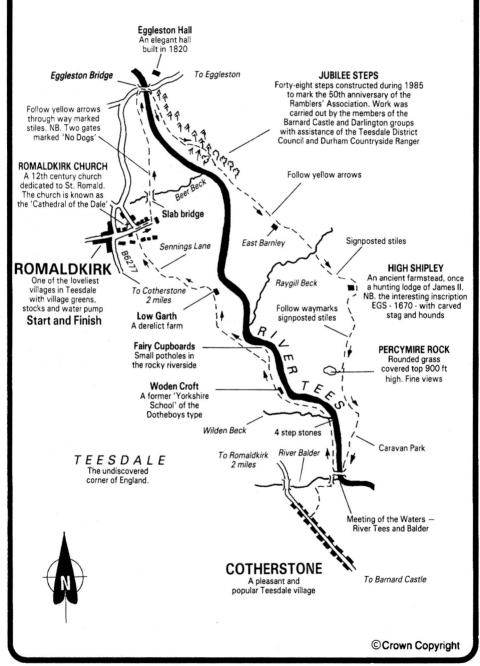

Eggleston Hall
An elegant hall
built in 1820

Eggleston Bridge

To Eggleston

JUBILEE STEPS
Forty-eight steps constructed during 1985
to mark the 50th anniversary of the
Ramblers' Association. Work was
carried out by the members of the
Barnard Castle and Darlington groups
with assistance of the Teesdale District
Council and Durham Countryside Ranger

Follow yellow arrows
through way marked
stiles. NB. Two gates
marked 'No Dogs'

Follow yellow arrows

ROMALDKIRK CHURCH
A 12th century church
dedicated to St. Romald.
The church is known as
the 'Cathedral of the Dale'

Beer Beck

Slab bridge

East Barnley

Signposted stiles

HIGH SHIPLEY
An ancient farmstead, once
a hunting lodge of James II.
NB. the interesting inscription
EGS - 1670 - with carved
stag and hounds

ROMALDKIRK
One of the loveliest
villages in Teesdale
with village greens,
stocks and water pump
Start and Finish

Sennings Lane

Raygill Beck

*To Cotherstone
2 miles*

Low Garth
A derelict farm

Follow waymarks
signposted stiles

PERCYMIRE ROCK
Rounded grass
covered top 900 ft
high. Fine views

Fairy Cupboards
Small potholes in
the rocky riverside

R I V E R   T E E S

Woden Croft
A former 'Yorkshire
School' of the
Dotheboys type

Wilden Beck

4 step stones

Caravan Park

TEESDALE
The undiscovered
corner of England.

*To Romaldkirk
2 miles*

River Balder

Meeting of the Waters —
River Tees and Balder

COTHERSTONE
A pleasant and
popular Teesdale village

To Barnard Castle

N

21. Romaldkirk

Route: *Romaldkirk — Eggleston Bridge — Jubilee Steps — High Shipley — Cotherstone — Woden Croft — Romaldkirk.*
Distance: *7 miles (11.2 km Fairly easy. Allow 3/4 hours.*
O.S. Maps: *Landranger Sheet 92 Outdoor Leisure 31.*
Parking: *Limited roadside parking in Romaldkirk. No parking on the village greens, please.*
Public Transport: *United: Service 75 Darlington — Middleton in Teesdale.*
Refreshments: *Kirk Inn, Rose and Crown, Romaldkirk; Fox and Hounds, Red Lion, Cotherstone.*
Note: *Between Romaldkirk and Eggleston Bridge there are two notices fixed on gates which state "No Dogs". Please observe the farmer's request.*

Discover the delights of Teesdale with an interesting round trip from Romaldkirk which includes the Jubilee Steps; historic High Shipley, plus Percymire Rock; Woden Croft of Yorkshire Schools fame and the Fairy Cupboards. This splendid seven-mile circuit on both sides of the River Tees offers superb views up and down Teesdale.

Start outside the delightful 12th century Romaldkirk Church known as the Cathedral of the Dale and go down to the bottom of the village green. Just beyond Greensend, turn left into a footpath signposted narrow walled path. Go down this and at the bottom, cross the slab bridge over Beer Beck. Turn right and cross the waymarked stile in the wall, left of a gate marked "No Dogs". Walk forward along the field and aim half right up to a corner wall stile with a waymark post right of a telegaph pole. Go diagonally over the next two waymarked stiled pastures of Hewcroft Hill with fine views of the elegant Eggleston Hall built in 1820. Exit through a gate marked "No Dogs" and turn right along the B6281 to cross the medieval Eggleston Bridge over the River Tees.

Beyond the bridge, cross the footpath signposted ladder stile and stride out for 400 yards along the private access road, the concrete building at the road end is the Tees Outlet, where water from the Kielder Reservoir reaches the River Tees. Do not go to the very end of the access road, but turn left over a ladder stile and in yards, cross a second stile marked "Footpath" to enter Great Wood. Climb steeply up the woodland by a series of 48 steps made from railway sleepers, called the Jubilee Steps. These steps were constructed during 1985 to mark the 50th anniversary of the Ramblers' Association. Work was carried out by members of the Darlington and Barnard Castle Groups with the assistance of the Teesdale District Council and Durham Countryside Rangers.

Leave the wood by a waymarked gate and turn right along the rough pasture aiming for an inset stile in the facing wall. Go diagonally up the next field, exit through a waymarked gate and pass East Barnley Farm on your right. A waymarked telegraph pole directs you straight on through a

gate in the facing wall. Bear half left and make your way over the ridge to a stone wall stile at the head of the wooded Raygill. Cross the stile and walk straight on to cross a similar signposted stile and bear half left up the field, via a waymarked telegraph pole and follow the track to High Shipley, an ancient farmstead, once a hunting lodge of James II.

The farm has an interesting datestone — 1670 EGS — with a carved stag and hounds. Outside the farm, go right along the road for a few yards, then turn right through a gate and follow the waymarks down by the plantation. Fork left along the rough pasture and cross the corner signposted stile. Go over the duckboard bridge and follow the waymark posts along the rough pasture valley. Once through a signposted gate, walk straight on and cross a slab bridge over the beck and turn left and follow the level path which contours round and goes downhill through a corner gate with a triple footpath sign. Follow the path round by the wall, where a short detour through a slit stile gives access to the rounded top of Percymire Rock, a fine viewpoint. From this lofty spot, admire the panoramic views of Teesdale overlooking the charming village of Cotherstone dominated by St Cuthbert's Church. There are westward views of Baldersdale with the twin tops of Goldsborough (1,274ft) and Shacklesborough (1,489ft.) on Cotherstone Moor.

Retrace your steps and go down the same field above the wooded beck, where a corner wall stile admits you into Shipley Wood. Keep within the edge of the wood, exit through a stile and stride downhill to the caravan site below. Go straight on over the site, cross a large stile by a gate and follow the broad track downhill which leads to the popular picnic spot by the River Tees. Cross the bridge of the River Tees and if you wish to have refreshments, turn left, cross the bridge over the River Balder for a stiff climb up to the charming village of Cotherstone, which boasts a couple of pubs.

For the return route to Romaldkirk, after crossing the bridge over the Tees, turn right along the

(Continued on page 90)

(Continued from page 89)

wooded riverside and up to your left, cross a waymarked stile. Turn right and follow the path round the field and cross a stile in the same field fence. Yards up river, cross four concrete step stones over the Wilden Beck. Up to your left, cross a stile and bear half right up a long field to pass the high walled old Woden Croft Summerhouse on your left. Onwards, pass in front of Woden Croft reputed to have been one of the Yorkshire Schools of the Dotheboys Hall type. Beyond the farm buildings, follow the track by the fence and the inset gate on your right, gives an extension woodland walk down to the Fairy Cupboards, pot holes and indentations in the rocky riverside. Retrace your steps and turn half right over the field to pass an unusual stone building with a blocked arched window, reputed to have been the resting place for travelling monks between Egglestone Abbey and Romaldkirk.

Climb the field path, high above the wooded riverside and turn right through a waymarked metal gate, wedged between two wooden gates. Go left, aim through a squeeze gate, walk straight on, cross a dried up stream and turn immediately right to cross a waymarked stile by a gate. Go along the field, pass the derelict Low Garth and follow the track half way round to turn up through a tiny gate in the hedge up on your right. Go diagonally over the next two pastures to enter Sennings Lane and follow this back to Romaldkirk to complete a satisfactory excursion on the delights of Teesdale.

A view from the Weardale Way out of Killhope.

Meander from Middleton in Teesdale to Gibson's Cave.

Church gateway at Wensley on the walk from Leyburn.

Riverside views on the path from Jervaulx Abbey.

22. Middleton in Teesdale

Route: *Middleton in Teesdale — Newbiggin — Bowlees — High Force — Low Force — Scoberry Bridge — Middleton in Teesdale.*
Distance: *About 10 miles (16km). Fairly easy to moderate. Allow 5/6 hours. Field and riverside paths with some road walking.*
O.S. Maps: *Landranger Sheet 92; Pathfinder Sheet NY82/92; Outdoor Leisure Sheet 31.*
Parking: *Car park in front of Hill Terrace, Middleton in Teesdale.*
Public transport: *United Service Darlington-Barnard Castle-Middleton in Teesdale.*
Refreshments: *Pubs, hotels, cafe and fish shop in Middleton in Teesdale. High Force Hotel.*
Note: *Those visiting High Force waterfall do so at their own risk and will indemnify Lord Barnard, the Upper Teesdale Estate and its employees against any claims of whatever nature arising in connection with their visits. Visitors are advised to wear substantial footwear. Please keep to the paths. Dogs must be under strict control.*

For the finest waterfall walk in England, try this loop in 'the land of the waterfalls', better known as Upper Teesdale. This walk visits three of Teesdale's well known waterfalls and returns along part of the popular Pennine Way, England's oldest long distance footpath.

From Middleton in Teesdale car park, turn left, pass the cast iron drinking fountain erected in 1875 and cross Bridge Street. Follow the B6277 along the Market Place and after crossing the bridge over the Hudeshope Beck, leave the B6277 and walk up the steep road signed 'Middleside', known as The Hude.

At the top, note the Clock Tower and the cobbled Lead Yard, a reminder of bygone lead mining days. Further on, pass Middleton House, built in 1815, which was the headquarters of the London Lead Mining Company until 1905. Today it's used by grouse shooting parties. Follow this road uphill for two miles which is fairly free from traffic, except for farm vehicles. There are excellent views over Teesdale. On the way, you will pass the hillside farms of Lanehead, Middle Side, Bell Farm and Ravelin Farm. At the road sign, 'No Through Road', turn left down the steep Miry Lane into the village of Newbiggin, boasting the oldest chapel in Methodism.

Follow the road behind Newbiggin and uphill, take the signposted path through the stile by the gate on your left. You will encounter plenty of mud as you progress over a couple of waymarked stiled/gated fields to pass behind the terraced cottages of Hood Gill. Continue by the field edge, go through a waymarked gate, and cross the centre of the next field and turn down the track to Bowlees Picnic Area, a popular spot at any time of the year. Upstream, follow the nature trail to see the spectacular Summerhill Force tumbling over Gibson's Cave, once the hiding place of Gibson, a 16th century outlaw who took refuge from the law. From the picnic area, cross Bowlees Beck and follow the path for 100 yards to Bowlees Visitor Centre housed in the former chapel.

Pass in front of the centre and go forward through the gate signposted 'Public Bridleway'.

The Wynch Bridge near Low Force

Follow the gated bridleway uphill, which used to be Teesdale's main road from Forest to Middleton until 1820. (Please close all gates, the second one is marked 'Beware of Bull'). At Ash Hill, a whitewashed farm cottage at 1,105ft above sea level, admire the extensive views of Upper Teesdale.

It's all downhill to the cluster of farm cottages of Dirt Pit meaning Deerpath, where the monks of Rievaulx Abbey maintained a chapel for the forest keepers when the deer roamed the Teesdale Forest. Pass between the cottages, cross the bridge over Ettersgill Beck, turn left to the Ettersgill Road, where opposite, cross a signposted stile over the open meadow. It's very boggy as you climb up the field to a gate in a nearby whitewashed barn. Cross another field, go through the gate and turn left to cross the corner signposted stile to enter the popular picnic area and car park at High Force. Those in need of refreshment should call at the High Force Hotel for bar meals.

Opposite the hotel, pay your admission for a woodland walk to High Force — England's finest waterfall. Take heed of the warnings. Back at the B6277, turn down the road and at the sign "No Footway", use the recently restored path (signposted/waymarked) down through the wooded whinstone crag, via an impressive flight of stone steps to the Tees and along the riverside to Holwick Head Bridge. This new "Crag Path"
(Continued on page 97)

22. Middleton in Teesdale

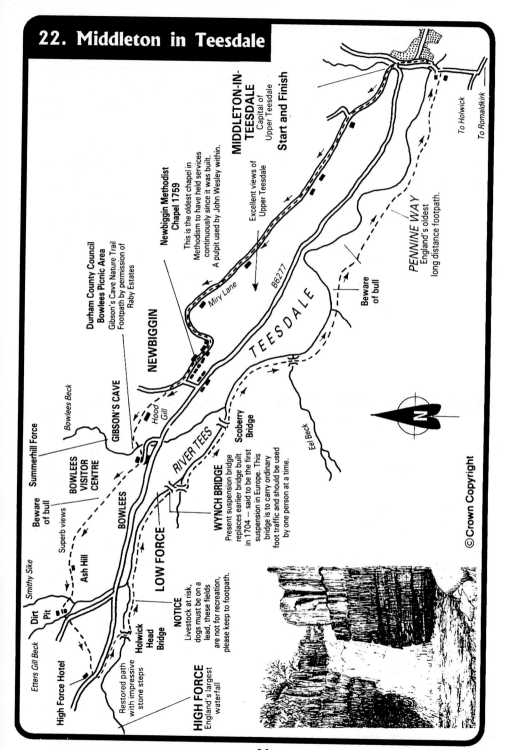

MIDDLETON-IN-TEESDALE
Capital of Upper Teesdale
Start and Finish

To Holwick

To Romaldkirk

Excellent views of Upper Teesdale

Newbiggin Methodist Chapel 1759
This is the oldest chapel in Methodism to have held services continuously since it was built. A pulpit used by John Wesley within.

Durham County Council Bowlees Picnic Area
Gibson's Cave Nature Trail Footpath by permission of Raby Estates

Miry Lane

B6277

T E E S D A L E

NEWBIGGIN

Beware of bull

PENNINE WAY
England's oldest long distance footpath.

Bowlees Beck

GIBSON'S CAVE

Hood Gill

Summerhill Force

BOWLEES VISITOR CENTRE

Beware of bull

Superb views

RIVER TEES

BOWLEES

Scoberry Bridge

Eel Beck

WYNCH BRIDGE
Present suspension bridge replaces earlier bridge built in 1704 — said to be the first suspension in Europe. This bridge is to carry ordinary foot traffic and should be used by one person at a time.

N

Smithy Sike

Etters Gill Beck

Dirt Pit

LOW FORCE

Ash Hill

Holwick Head Bridge

NOTICE
Livestock at risk, dogs must be on a lead, these fields are not for recreation, please keep to footpath.

Restored path with impressive stone steps

HIGH FORCE
England's largest waterfall

High Force Hotel

©**Crown Copyright**

(Continued from page 95)

avoids 600 yards of road walking along the B6277. Cross Holwick Head Bridge over the River Tees. The walk now follows the Pennine Way throughout the return route to Middleton in Teesdale. Although detailed direction is not necessary for the next couple of miles or more, you are reminded to keep to the paths and keep dogs on a lead. With the River Tees as your constant companion, follow the pleasant stiled riverside path and a mile downstream you will reach Salmon Leap, better known as Low Force or Little Force. Below this popular waterfall is Wynch Bridge, a chain suspension bridge nicknamed the 'Two Inch Bridge' which replaced Europe's first suspension.

Follow the Pennine Way by the Tees and note the views of Holwick Lodge and Holwick Village. About 880 yards further on pass the slender Scoberry Bridge and continue downstream until you reach a ladder stile in the fence on your right where you leave the river. Cross this, bear left and

negotiate the slippery step stones and over another ladder stile; cross the metal footbridge over the beck. Climb up the wooded hillside, turn left and at the top of Unthank Bank, you will encounter plenty of ankle deep mud. Continue, hug the fence, and at the end of the field cross the stile and follow the lovely green path down through a stile by a gate.

Cross Unthank Beck by Park End Wood and in this stiled field watch out for the bull. In the next field, a double Pennine Way sign directs you along by a low ruined wall and over a stile, where in the adjoining field you will see another bull. Eventually you will enter the narrow walled lane (very watery) known as The Old Holwick Road which was the ancient route from Laithkirk to Holwick. Proceed over some more stiled fields to join the cart road which leads you out onto the B6277 road between the cattle mart and British Telecom. Turn left along the road, cross Middleton Bridge and back to Middleton in Teesdale to end a very satisfying walk.

The disused Skittswood Pumping Station, used until 1960's to pump water to Brancepeth Colliery

PAGE BANK
A former pit village — only four houses remain.

To Brancepeth

Page Bank Bridge

Monument
A replica of a coal wagon on a concrete plinth, erected in 1976 to commemorate the Rocking Strike of 1863, the forerunner of the checkweight system.

Jubilee Bridge Picnic Area

To Brandon

WILLINGTON

Whitworth Church
Founded about 1183 first known incumbent 1427

RIVER WEAR

Whitworth Hall
Once the home of Bobby Shafto

Sunnybrow
A former colliery village

Lowfield Farm

Whitworth Road

Holy Well Burn

Jubilee Bridge

Views to Brancepeth Castle

Byers Green

Hagg Lane

To Middlestone Moor

Sunnybrow Bridge
A girder bridge known as the 'Pay Bridge'

Beck

Hagg Farm

Alternative Path

Hemlington

Todhills

Turn left leave the lane

Newfield

Furness Mill Farm

Old pipe works

Leave the railway walk at the wooden bench seat and follow field/woodland walk to river.

New Monkey
(Free House-Restaurant)

Old Park Terrace
(a single terrace)

Join the Auckland Walk

Byers Green picnic area

BINCHESTER ROCKS
A long street of terraced houses

Old station platform

The former Hunwick railway station (private)

Two long distance walks - The Wear Valley Way and The Weardale Way follow part of the railway track

Bellburn Wood

Auckland Walk
A five mile railway walk from New Coundon to Spennymoor

The Bishop - Brandon Walk
A popular railway walk of 9½ miles from Bishop to Brandon. In 1976 the walk was opened to the public. The railway line was opened in 1875 and closed 20th June 1966.

Bishop — Brandon Walk (Dismantled Railway)

Dismantled Railway

Binchester Roman Fort

Lodge Farm

Follow yellow waymarks

Stone bridge over disused railway line

Between the second and third stone bridges, climb the signposted steps and follow the waymarks over the second bridge

Newton Cap Viaduct
Built 1856-57

Jocks Bridge

To Crook A689

To New Coundon

Newton Cap Bridge
Two arches with different shapes. Built in 1388

Auckland Park

River Gaunless

N

Bondgate Car Park
Start and Finish

BISHOP AUCKLAND
A historic market town

98

23. Bishop Auckland

Route: *Bishop Auckland — New Monkey — Furness Mill Farm — Jubilee Bridge — Page Bank — Hagg Lane — Auckland Walk — Bishop Auckland.*
Distance: *Over 9 miles (14.5km) Allow 5 hours. Moderate. Easy to follow.*
O.S. Maps: *Landranger Sheets 92 and 93. Pathfinder Sheet NZ 13; NZ 23/33 (581).*
Public Transport: *Buses: Regular services from most places to Bishop Auckland. Trains: Saltburn — Middlesbrough — Darlington — Bishop Auckland.*
Refreshments: *Pubs, cafes, hotels in Bishop Auckland. New Monkey, Hunwick, Brown Trout, Sunnybrow.*
Note: *Expect plenty of mud.*

Railway walks in County Durham are very popular. Walk the line along a couple of railway walks, linked with a riverside ramble for a great circuit based on Bishop Auckland in South West Durham.

From Bondgate car park in Bishop Auckland, turn right along High Bondgate and by the Newton Cap pub, descend Bridge Street, bear half right to reach the old railway line for the start of the Bishop—Brandon Walk, one of the best railway walks in the county. Follow the line across the impressive ten arch Newton Cap Viaduct over the River Wear and admire the extensive views. Continue along the reclaimed railway for 1½ miles to the former railway station at Hunwick, where the New Monkey pub offers meals and drinks.

From Hunwick Station (private), follow the old railway for about half a mile and look out for a bench seat on your left, where you leave the railway walk. If you miss this turn off continue on until a public footpath sign directs you down a track and where it bends right, walk forward through a facing stile and go down the field edge along a wooded beckside path to reach the River Wear.

To continue the main route, opposite the seat go down the unsignposted stepped path, through a kissing gate and diagonally over a couple of fields into the wood for a steep, slippery walk via the mill race to the river. Pass Furness Mill Farm and follow the riverside path to Sunnybrow Bridge, where both routes meet. This girder footbridge is known locally as the ''Pay Bridge''.

An interesting diversion here is to go up the hillside to Sunnybrow and see the replica of a coal wagon on a concrete plinth erected in 1976 to commemorate the Rocking Strike of 1863, the forerunner of the checkweight system. It's also a good excuse to call in at the Brown Trout for drinks.

From the monument, return downhill for a pleasant riverside stroll eastwards to reach the Jubilee Bridge picnic area. Note, the Jubilee Bridge was built for Queen Victoria's Golden Jubilee in 1887.

Cross over the busy road, pass the sewage works and follow the rutted riverside path behind the disused brick building (Skittswood Pumping Station) which was used until the 1960s to pump water to Brancepeth Colliery. Beyond this building go through a kissing gate and where the river curves right (check map) leave the river and aim half left above hawthorn bushes. At the corner fence, turn left and hug the hedge all the way to Lowfields Farm, where in front of the houses, turn right along the field edge. At the river, turn left through a kissing gate and head eastwards (detailed direction not necessary) along the gated track for more than a mile or more, with the River Wear your constant companion, to reach the former pit village of Page Bank.

Cross Page Bank Bridge over the River Wear and walk up the steep Whitworth Road for half a mile to pass the entrance of Whitworth Hall, totally rebuilt in 1877 after a fire. This was the ancestral home of Bobby Shafto, of ballad fame.

Opposite Whitworth Church entrance, cross the road into Hagg Lane (footpath signposted) and follow this delightful hedgerowed lane with extensive views over the Wear Valley to Brancepeth Castle. Go down past Hagg Farm and where the lane bends right, turn sharp left up the path by the hedge on your left. At the top, cross a railway line by Old Park Terrace.

You have now joined the Auckland Walk, another attractive railway walk from Spennymoor to New Coundon. Turn right along the track bed for half a mile and cross the road to reach the Byers Green picnic area. Follow this railway walk by the former Byers Green Station to cross over the Binchester Road and head southwards past Binchester Rocks for a delightful walk of a mile or more. You will go under two impressive stone bridges and as you reach the third bridge, turn left up the stepped path (signposted Auckland Park and Binchester Roman Fort) and left along the embankment to cross a waymarked stile.

Turn left over the second bridge and follow the yellow waymarks down the next four stiled/gated fields by the boundary wall of Auckland Park to come out onto the road near the River Wear. Turn left, cross Jock's Bridge where the River Gaunless meets the River Wear, and follow the road with an impressive view of Auckland Castle, residence of the Bishop of Durham. Turn up the steep Wear Chare to complete one of the best walks in this book, back to Bishop Auckland.

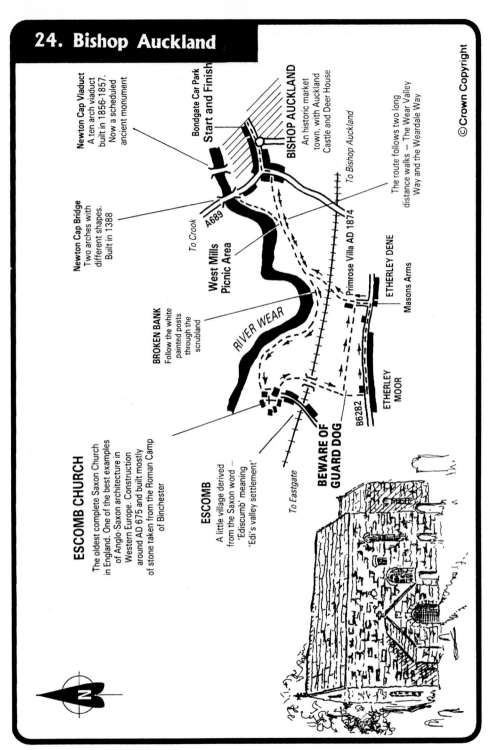

24. Bishop Auckland

© Crown Copyright

Newton Cap Viaduct
A ten arch viaduct built in 1856-1857. Now a scheduled ancient monument

Bondgate Car Park Start and Finish

BISHOP AUCKLAND
An historic market town, with Auckland Castle and Deer House

To Bishop Auckland

The route follows two long distance walks — The Wear Valley Way and the Weardale Way

Newton Cap Bridge
Two arches with different shapes. Built in 1388

To Crook

A689

West Mills Picnic Area

BROKEN BANK
Follow the white painted posts through the scrubland

RIVER WEAR

Primrose Villa AD 1874

ETHERLEY DENE

Masons Arms

ETHERLEY MOOR

B6282

BEWARE OF GUARD DOG

To Eastgate

ESCOMB CHURCH

The oldest complete Saxon Church in England. One of the best examples of Anglo-Saxon architecture in Western Europe. Construction around AD 675 and built mostly of stone taken from the Roman Camp of Binchester

ESCOMB

A little village derived from the Saxon word — 'Ediscumb' meaning 'Edi's valley settlement'

N

100

24. Bishop Auckland

Route: *Bishop Auckland — West Mill Picnic Area — Broken Bank — Escomb — Primrose Hill — Bishop Auckland.*
Distance: *About 4 miles (6.5km). Easy. Allow 2/3 hours.*
O.S. Maps: *Landranger Sheets 92 and 93.*
Parking: *Bondgate car park, Bishop Auckland.*
Public Transport: *Any bus to Bishop Auckland. Trains from Darlington to Bishop Auckland.*
Refreshments: *Plenty of pubs, hotels and cafes in Bishop Auckland. Saxon Inn, Escomb; Mason's Arms, Etherley Dene.*

Your objective on this Wear Valley walk is Escomb Church, which is the oldest complete Saxon church in England.

This short stroll starts and finishes from Bondgate car park in Bishop Auckland. Leave the car park, turn right along North Bondgate into High Bondgate and cross the A689 into West Road and right into Hexham Street. At the street end (footpath sign missing) go down the path between the allotments to come out almost opposite West Mill Picnic Area. Here you join not one but two long distance walks — the Wear Valley Way and the Weardale Way, both follow the outward route to Escomb.

Turn left along the road by some more allotments, noting the West Mills Playing Fields, located on the reclaimed area of the Dam and the Weir. At the end of the road, cross a Public Footpath signposted stile and follow the path round by the River Wear and up through the scrubland of gorse and hawthorn known as Broken Bank with waymarked white painted posts. Look back to "Bishop" for views of Newton Cap Bridge and viaduct. When the path splits by a waymarked post near a bench seat, take the lower path on your right and proceed westwards until another waymarked post directs you back down to the river. Turn left along the riverside and in yards, cross a footbridge over a rust-coloured stream. Follow the path along the pleasant riverside pastures for the best part of the walk. After four fields, cross a stile, veer left and right along by a mound of scrubland and out into a lane by the railed electricity sub station. Turn up the lane by the children's play area, via Dunelm Chare, into the small village of Escomb, renowned for its simple Saxon church which is well worth a visit.

Escomb Church is regarded as one of the finest and most complete early Saxon churches in England, although its origins are shrouded in the

The simple Saxon church at Escomb

proverbial mists of antiquity. It could date from the seventh century. The church is built of stones from the Roman fort of Binchester.

At the east end of Escomb, leave by Bede Close, cross the unsignposted stile and turn right southwards up the edge of the next two stiled fields with good views of the Wear Valley. Cross the bridge over the Weardale Railway with an interesting North Eastern Railway notice. Continue up the next two stiled fields into Green Lane where by the shed marked "Beware of the Guard Dog" you can turn left along the fields via kissing gates and stiles to Primrose Hill or go up Green Lane to Etherley Moor. Turn left by South View and follow the footway by the B6282 to Etherley Dene where, opposite the Mason's Arms, turn left along the unsurfaced lane to the terraced cottages of Primrose Villa AD 1874, marked Primrose Hill on the O.S. map.

The lane leads you down over the Weardale Railway and across the stile opposite. Turn right and follow the path which brings you back to Broken Bank for a return by the outward route, except at West Mills Picnic Area, you can follow the riverside road to the A689 and walk up Newton Cap Bank back to Bishop Auckland.

© Crown Copyright

Middlehope Shield Mine. Extensive old lead mine workings. Dangerous - do not explore

Old mine entrance railed and sealed

Redundant reservoir

Weardale Way. – A 78 mile walk from Monkwearmouth to Cowshill

Slit Mine Extensive old lead mine workings Dangerous — do not explore

High Mill. - An old cornmill. Private land and garden - keep to footpath. Keep dogs on leash

To Stanhope

WESTGATE An old world, stone built village

Ford - subject to flash floods

Middlehope Burn

RIVER WEAR

Ford and footbridge

Short cut

Waterfall

The old Weardale Railway (opened 1895 - closed 1961). NOTICE - This property is private. No right of way exists for any class of traffic. This notice relates to the dismantled railway near the right of way between Westgate to Daddryshield

Seeingsike Road. (A walled stony track) Public bridleway - once the route for carrier galloways bearing lead ore to the Rookhope Mill

Triple footpath signpost

Fine views

Side Head. A tiny farming hamlet

Side Head Farm

An elevated dead end road with extensive views over Weardale

W E A R D A L E (Valley of the Prince Bishops)

DADDRYSHIELD A tiny hamlet, infamous for its past cock-fighting contests

Ford and footbridge

WEARDALE WAY

Stiff climb

Steep railed steps

Ponderlane Bridge

To Cowshill

Harthope Burn

To Langdon Beck

A689

Ford and footbridge

ST. JOHN'S CHAPEL A lovely little village with a town hall built 1865 and restored 1952. Derives its name from its parish church, dedicated to St John the Baptist. Founded 1465, rebuilt 1752. **Start and Finish**

The joint highest classified road in England and Wales - 2056 ft

N

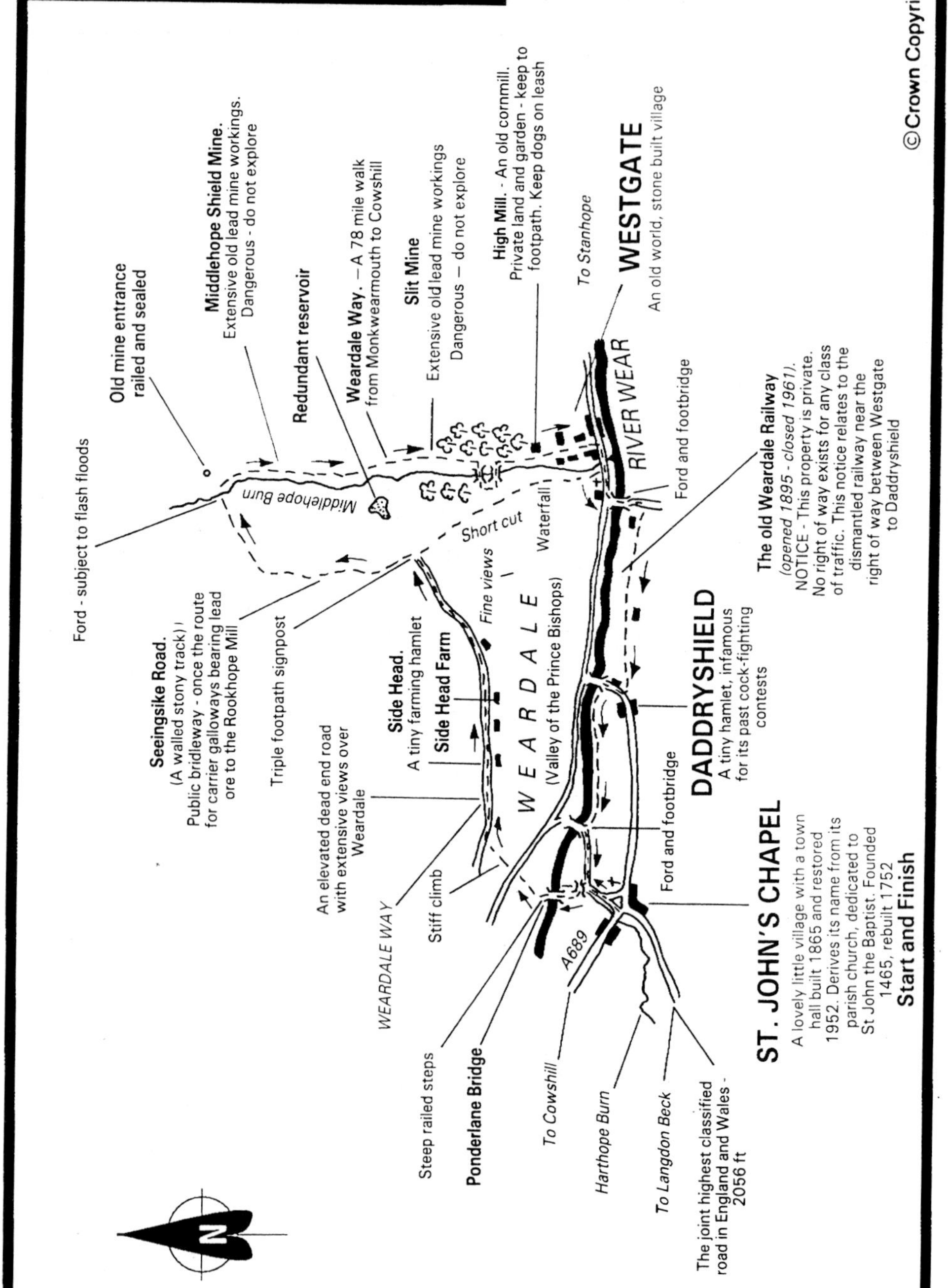

25. St John's Chapel

Route: *St John's Chapel — Side Head — Westgate — Daddry Shield — St John's Chapel.*
Distance: *Over 5 miles (8km). Moderate with a couple of climbs.*
O.S.Maps: *Landranger Sheets 87, 92. Outdoor Leisure 31.*
Parking: *Market Square, St John's Chapel.*
Public Transport: *Weardale Motor Services Ltd. Services 101/102. Bishop Auckland — Cowshill Sunday; change at Stanhope every other day.*
Refreshments: *The King's Arms Hotel; The King's Head Hotel; Golden Lion; Blue Bell Inn, St John's Chapel. Hare and Hounds, Westgate.*
Warning: *The Middlehope Beck is subject to flash floods and can be difficult to ford after heavy rain. Do not explore the old lead mines. The ruined buildings are dangerous and unsafe. The disused Weardale Railway is private property and no right of way exists. Please keep dogs on a leash.*

This high and low level walk from St John's Chapel provides a fine introduction to Upper Weardale. Using part of the Weardale Way, it links St John's Chapel with Side Head and journeys down the delightful Middlehope Burn — an amateur industrial archaeologists' and botanists' paradise — to the charming village of Westgate for a low-level pasture path and riverside return.

Leave St John's Chapel by the lane behind the Town Hall and follow this to reach a row of cottages. Turn left, cross the bridge over the Harthope Burn and by the Public Footpath signpost turn right and follow the paved path to cross Ponderlane Bridge over the River Wear. Walk forward up the fieldside to climb some steep railed steps and up the next field, aim diagonally for the signposted stone wall stile to come out on to the road. Almost opposite, take the signposted path, diagonally up two more stiled pastures for a stiff climb up to the next road. This ascent is rewarded with unfolding views of Upper Weardale.

Turn right along the hillside road, virtually traffic free except for farm vehicles, and pass through the hamlet of Side Head with its few farms and holiday cottages. From this elevated road there are extensive views of Weardale's surrounding summits with Westgate and Daddry Shield below.

After a mile the road ends with a triple footpath signpost at the junction of Seeingsike Road, an old highway once used by lead miners and carrier galloways. For a short cut to Westgate, take the path through the first gate on your right and walk down to the village below.

For the main route, turn left up the walled Seeingsike Road, a stony track which climbs, twists and turns up the empty fell with only grazing cattle and sheep, plus a redundant reservoir and dotted ruined buildings. After nearly 880 yards, at a height of 1,340 feet and where the track turns left, take the right fork, another walled track which plunges steeply down into the valley of the Middlehope Burn. At the bottom, go through the gate and ford the Middlehope Burn, if you can, as it might be difficult after heavy wet weather. If it

is impossible to cross the burn, retrace your steps and use the short cut to Westgate.

Once over the burn, bear half right, avoid the watery bog and pass the gated old lead mine on your left. Head southwards along the bottom of the valley of the Middlehope Burn to pass between the extensive lead mine ruined remains of Middlehope Shield Mine with bridge abutments and buildings visible. Stay on the left of the burn and make your way along the valley on an even contour above the derelict buildings with unfenced walls and deep drops — so be careful.

Follow the path along the wooded burn to reach Slit Mine with more evidence of Weardale's bygone lead mining industry. The mine shaft at 585ft was one of the deepest in the North — thank goodness, it's now capped. Remember old lead mines are dangerous, so do not explore. Continue downstream, skirt round the old buildings and beyond the dressing floors, go through a white gate into the charming Slitts Wood, a well-known beauty spot and nature reserve, noted for its fauna and flora. You will cross and recross the burn by a couple of footbridges and once through a kissing gate, note the pretty waterfalls as you proceed along the private garden path of High Mill, an old corn mill, to enter the charming village of Westgate, once a centre for cock fighting.

Turn right along the main street (A689) and just beyond the garage, turn left along the lane to cross the footbridge over the River Wear. Walk up the road between the abutment ends of the old Weardale Railway (opened 1895, closed 1961) and in yards, take the signposted path on your right and pass the three terraced cottages. Go through the corner gate and proceed westwards across three pastures to the nine terraced cottages of Windyside. Note, the nearby old railway line is private property and no right of way exists. Pass in front of the cottages and at the far end, note the model miniature stone cottage, water wheel and bridge. Turn right, go under the washing lines and left over a footbridge plus ladder stile and back out into the pasture. Do not

(Continued on page 104)

103

(Continued from page 103)

take the route by the river, it's the old railway line and not a right of way.

Climb up and go through the gate wedged between the wall and wood to follow the path along the wooded field edge. Cross the stile in the wall on your right and turn left along the stiled path into the hamlet of Daddry Shield, another place noted for its past cock fighting contests.

Turn right along the A689 to Daddry Shield Bridge with its signposted path and go down the steps to the riverside. Follow the river upstream for one of the best waterside walks in Weardale with plenty of pretty waterfalls. After 880 yards, you reach Huntshield with its ford and footbridge. Do not cross the footbridge, but turn left and follow the lane back to St John's Chapel to complete a lovely little walk in Weardale.

26. Killhope and the Carriers' Way

Route: *Killhope Wheel — Allenheads — Cowshill — Low Rush — Killhope Wheel.*
Distance: *Over 10 miles (18km). Strenuous. Allow 6 hours.*
O.S.Maps: *Landranger Sheet 87, Pathfinder Sheet NY 84/94*
Parking: *Free car park, Killhope Wheel Lead Mining Centre, Upper Weardale.*
Public Transport: *Weardale Motor Services Ltd. Summer Sunday service only from May to September. Check times with bus company. Alternatively, use Service 101 from Bishop Auckland to Cowshill for a two-mile road walk along the A689 to Killhope.*
Refreshments: *Allenheads Inn, The Hemmel Coffee Shop, Allenheads. Cowshill Hotel, The Calf House, Cowshill.*
Warning: *Do not attempt in adverse weather conditions. Map and compass essential. Danger — extensive tree felling operations may be in progress in the forest of the Weardale Estate. Dogs should be kept on leads.*

Using the Carriers' Way, this forest, fell and field walk is a tough trek that links wild Weardale with the secluded valley of East Allendale and visits Allenheads, the highest village in England.

Before you set out, visit the Killhope Wheel Lead Mining Centre (admission charge) which is the best preserved lead mining site in the North Pennines. See the lead mining museum with restored smithy, stables and miners' lodgings. There are working models and audio visual displays. View the Park Level, Lead Crushing Mill with its 34ft high water wheel known locally as Killhope Wheel.

From the car park, ford the Killhope Burn and cross the busy A689 to the waymarked gate opposite and enter the private forest of the Weardale Estate with an order that all dogs must be kept on leads. Follow the forest track steeply as it twists and turns northwards up Carriers' Hill with warning signs relating to the extensive tree felling operations in progress, so take care. At the top of the forest, cross a waymarked stile by a gate and walk forward out on to Middlehope Moor to the waymark corner fence. From this point, aim northwards over the moor and follow the 3ft high wooden marker posts, (eight in all) to traverse spongy moor, strewn with slime.

On the horizon, the highest point of the walk at 2,025 feet above sea level, you cross over the county boundary from Durham into Northumberland and admire the panoramic views. You can see the cairned summit of Killhope Law (2,208ft) and the highest Pennine peak of Cross Fell (2,903ft) with Great Dun Fell (2,780ft) easily recognised by its radar and weather masts. To the north, ahead of you is the lovely little valley of East Allendale, where patchwork pastures meet moorland, and further on you can see the distant Simonside and Cheviot Hills. Behind you are the lofty heights of Weardale with Chapelfell Top and Burnhope Seat both visible.

Go down moorland path to a short post with a yellow arrow to reach a broad green bridle track. You have now joined the Carriers' Way, an ancient packhorse highway between Weardale

and Allendale. It was used to take lead ore on ponies from Killhope to Allenheads Smelt Mill and then on to the port of Newcastle. Turn right and head down the track for a mile or more past the redundant Dodd Reservoir and use the arched flue path to go between the ruined remains of Allenheads Smelt Mill. Exit through the signposted gate "Killhope 3 miles" and cross Smelt Mill Bridge (1925) over the River East Allen.

Turn right and follow the road for a mile to the former lead mining village of Allenheads which claims to be the highest village in England. The once-forgotten village is today popular with its Heritage Centre including craft workshop, exhibition centre and trout farm which was visited

Robert Maddison

The 34ft high Killhope Wheel

by Prince Charles in February 1988. You must visit the popular Antiques Bar at the Allenheads Inn and see the memorabilia. Peter and Linda Stenson, owners of this old pub, built in 1770, welcome walkers.

From Allenheads, turn up the B6295 in the direction of Cowshill for unavoidable road walk of a mile, with a stiff climb up to the county boundary

(Continued on page 107)

26. Killhope

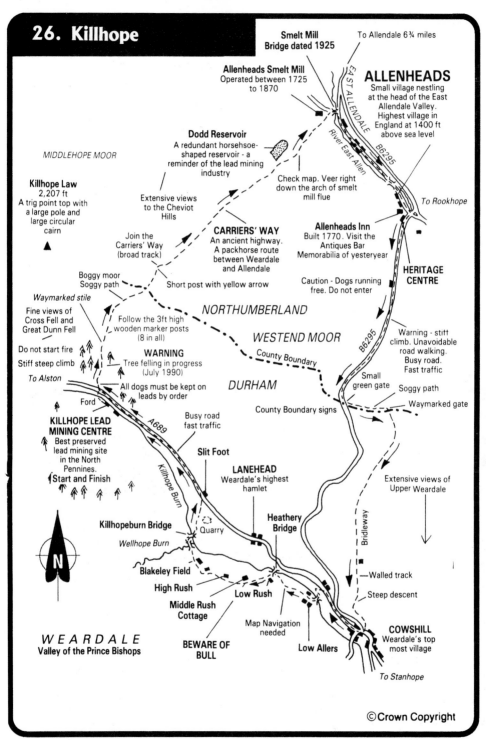

Smelt Mill
Bridge dated 1925

To Allendale 6¾ miles

Allenheads Smelt Mill
Operated between 1725
to 1870

ALLENHEADS
Small village nestling
at the head of the East
Allendale Valley.
Highest village in
England at 1400 ft
above sea level

Dodd Reservoir
A redundant horsehsoe-
shaped reservoir - a
reminder of the lead
mining industry

MIDDLEHOPE MOOR

EAST ALLENDALE

River East Allen

B6295

Check map. Veer right
down the arch of smelt
mill flue

Killhope Law
2,207 ft
A trig point top with
a large pole and
large circular
cairn

Extensive views
to the Cheviot
Hills

Join the
Carriers' Way
(broad track)

CARRIERS' WAY
An ancient highway.
A packhorse route
between Weardale
and Allendale

Allenheads Inn
Built 1770. Visit the
Antiques Bar
Memorabilia of yesteryear

To Rookhope

**HERITAGE
CENTRE**

Boggy moor
Soggy path

Short post with yellow arrow

Caution - Dogs running
free. Do not enter

Waymarked stile

Fine views of
Cross Fell and
Great Dunn Fell

Do not start fire

Stiff steep climb

To Alston

Ford

NORTHUMBERLAND

Follow the 3ft high
wooden marker posts
(8 in all)

WARNING
Tree felling in progress
(July 1990)

All dogs must be kept on
leads by order

WESTEND MOOR

County Boundary

DURHAM

County Boundary signs

B6295

Warning - stiff
climb. Unavoidable
road walking.
Busy road.
Fast traffic

Small
green gate

Soggy path

Waymarked gate

**KILLHOPE LEAD
MINING CENTRE**
Best preserved
lead mining site
in the North
Pennines.
Start and Finish

A689

Killhope Burn

Busy road
fast traffic

Slit Foot

LANEHEAD
Weardale's highest
hamlet

**Heathery
Bridge**

Extensive views of
Upper Weardale

Bridleway

N

Killhopeburn Bridge

Wellhope Burn

Quarry

Blakeley Field

High Rush

**Middle Rush
Cottage**

**BEWARE OF
BULL**

Low Rush

Map Navigation
needed

Low Allers

Walled track

Steep descent

COWSHILL
Weardale's top
most village

W E A R D A L E
Valley of the Prince Bishops

To Stanhope

(Continued from page 105)

between Northumberland and Durham at a height of 1,926 feet. Between the boundary signs, turn left through a small green gate in the wall and follow the boggy path eastwards by the waymarked wall/fence. Turn right through a hurdle gate (waymarked) and head south down Burtree Fell following the bridle path by the fence for 1½ miles. Admire the wonderful views of Weardale. The path becomes a walled track, as you descend steeply into Cowshill, Weardale's top most village with refreshments available at the Cowshill Hotel.

From Cowshill, turn right, westwards along either the lower village road or the A689 road, both meet and follow this until you reach a footpath sign opposite a couple of cottages. Turn left through the gate and zigzag down the track to cross Low Allers Bridge over the Killhope Burn. Turn right, pass between the three forlorn cottages of Low Allers and continue along the lower track that leads up through a gate. Walk to the far end of the next field, turn right through the wall gap and go straight on by the low wall to cross not one, but two stiles in the field corner.

Continue to the end of the watery meadow, cut through the ruined wall and bear right, diagonally down the fairly steep rough pasture to the Killhope Burn and along to Heathery Bridge which is double waymarked. Do not cross the bridge but turn up the track to pass Low Rush on your left. Turn right along the gated farm road and watch out for the grazing bull. Pass Middle Rush Cottage, walk westwards and beyond High Rush (under renovation), turn right through the wall gap and left along the gated track which leads past another isolated farmstead and onwards to pass in front of Blakey Field Farm. Go down the track, cross the bridge over the Wellhope Burn which joins the Killhope Burn and follow the lower track (do not turn left) to cross the Killhope Burn Bridge. Follow the track, turn right through a gate and go left up the hillside path to pass a disused quarry on your right and aim through a small red metal gate. Cut across the corner field and exit through a signposted gate to come out almost opposite Slit Foot House on the A689. Turn left along this busy main road for a mile to Killhope Wheel to end the tough trek.

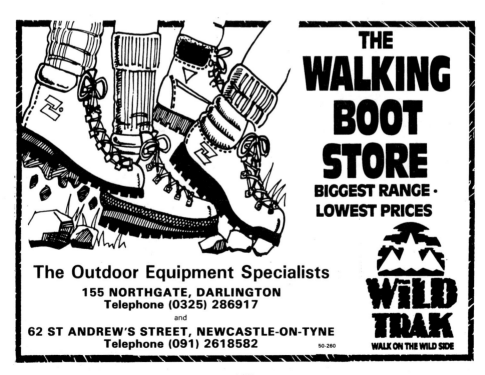

Step out from St John's Chapel for a view of Daddry Shield.

Underneath the arches — from Sunderland Bridge.

Ni-Trax ®

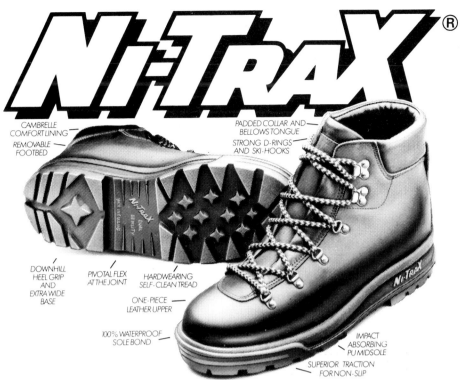

CAMBRELLE COMFORT LINING

REMOVABLE FOOTBED

PADDED COLLAR AND BELLOWS TONGUE

STRONG D-RINGS AND SKI-HOOKS

DOWNHILL HEEL GRIP AND EXTRA WIDE BASE

PIVOTAL FLEX AT THE JOINT

HARDWEARING SELF-CLEAN TREAD

ONE-PIECE LEATHER UPPER

100% WATERPROOF SOLE BOND

IMPACT ABSORBING PU MIDSOLE

SUPERIOR TRACTION FOR NON-SLIP

The Original High Specification
HIKING & COUNTRY FOOTWEAR

Presenting Ni-Trax, the all British walking boots that have been developed by experts, after exhaustive research into what experienced ramblers really want.

They feature a hi-tech Nitrile rubber outsole with a special polyurethane midsole, which, during manufacture, traps thousands of tiny air bubbles – and so offers you an outstanding shock absorbing, 100% waterproof and permanent sole bond.

Flexible and lightweight, Ni-Trax is a tremendous step forward in hiking footwear, it cuts down on foot fatigue, provides the ultimate in cushioned comfort, and doesn't even need breaking in.

Step in to Ni-trax walking boots and shoes – they're ahead of ordinary outdoor footwear by miles.

Available from Sizes 3 to 12 and in ½ sizes (Mens, Womens and childrens).

'Arran' Boot (C2 166) Dark Forest Green/Black collar and tongue.

'Tiree' Shoe (C2 168) Petrel/Mid Brown.

'Ross' Boot (C2326) Redwood/Black.

C2166

C2326

C2168

G. B. Britton Lodge Road, Kingswood, Bristol, BS15 1JB. Tel: (0272) 352777 Telex: 44273 Fax: (0272) 352107

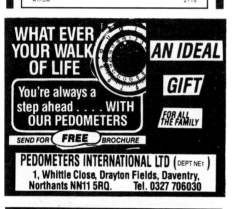

116

The Old Manor House Hotel

Accommodation

At the time the efforts of Colonel Robert and John were frowned upon and their Manor House and its lands were sequestered by Parliamentary decree for 'Royalist Activities' but returned along with the Barony to Robert in 1672.

Bars, Restaurant, Lounge

Conference Facilities

Leisure Complex

The Old Manor House Hotel

West Auckland, County Durham
Telephone Bishop Auckland 832504/832358. Telex 587485. Fax (0388) 833566

DARLINGTON
at the centre of the magic

A warm and friendly welcome awaits you in the charming market town of Darlington, winner of the 1989 Northumbria in Bloom Contest in The Small Cities Section. Darlington provides the ideal holiday base while visiting the Northumbria Region.

You can explore Darlington's Railway heritage boasting of the first ever public passenger steam railway in 1825, see Stephenson's original 'Locomotion' or enjoy James Heriot country and also the ancient castles and cathedrals, wild sweeping moorlands, sleepy dales, magnificent museums and enchanting villages.

With all of this and easy accessibility by train, bus, air, or car, Darlington is quite definitely 'At the Centre Of It All'

contact: Tourist Information Centre, Dolphin Centre, Horsemarket, Darlington, DL1 5QU, Tel: (0325) 382698

DARLINGTON CIVIC TRUST ONE OF THE UK'S TOP TEN TOWNS

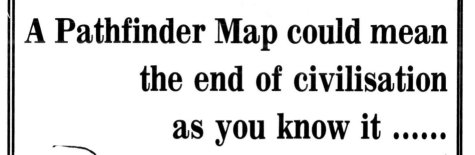

27. Sunderland Bridge

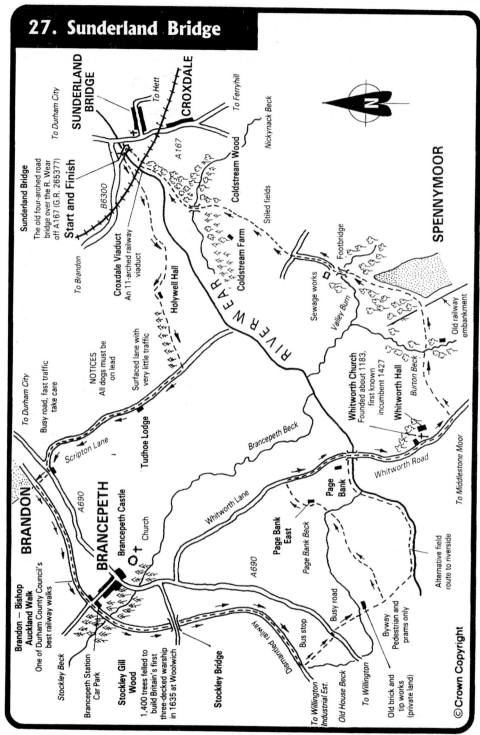

Sunderland Bridge
The old four-arched road bridge over the R. Wear off A167 (G.R. 265377)

Start and Finish

Croxdale Viaduct
An 11-arched railway viaduct

NOTICES
All dogs must be on lead

Surfaced lane with very little traffic

Busy road, fast traffic take care

Whitworth Church
Founded about 1183, first known incumbent 1427

Brandon – Bishop Auckland Walk
One of Durham County Council's best railway walks

Stockley Gill Wood
1,400 trees felled to build Britain's first three-decked warship in 1635 at Woolwich

To Hett
To Durham City
To Ferryhill
Nickynack Beck

SUNDERLAND BRIDGE
CROXDALE

A167
Coldstream Wood
Stiled fields
B6300

To Brandon

Holywell Hall
Coldstream Farm

Footbridge

SPENNYMOOR

Sewage works
Valley Burn
Burton Beck

Old railway embankment

To Durham City
Scripton Lane
Tudhoe Lodge
Brancepeth Beck

Whitworth Hall
Whitworth Road
To Middlestone Moor

BRANDON
A690
BRANCEPETH
Brancepeth Castle
Church

Whitworth Lane
Page Bank East
Page Bank Beck
Page Bank

Alternative field route to riverside

Stockley Beck
Brancepeth Station Car Park

Whitworth Lane
A690

Bus stop
Busy road

Byway Pedestrian and prams only

Stockley Bridge
Dismantled railway
Old House Beck
To Willington Industrial Est.
To Willington
Old brick and tip works (private land)

RIVER WEAR

122

27. Sunderland Bridge

Route: *Sunderland Bridge — Scripton Lane — Brandon/Bishop Walk — Page Bank — Whitworth Road — Valley Burn — Coldstream Wood — Sunderland Bridge.*
Distance: *About 11 miles (17½km). Moderate. Allow 5/5½ hours.*
O.S. Maps: *Landranger Sheet 93, Pathfinder Sheet NZ 23/33.*
Parking: *Sunderland Bridge (the old road bridge over the River Wear) Croxdale, off A167. G.R. 265377.*
Public Transport: *United: Northern and O.K. Travel pass Sunderland Bridge.*

Enjoy the peace and quiet of the Durham countryside with this good day's walk starting from the old Sunderland Bridge, near Croxdale. This pleasant walk uses bridleways and byways, via the Brandon/Bishop Walk, before crossing the River Wear for a return through fields, woods and riverside. From the north end of old Sunderland Bridge, take the signposted "Brancepeth-Bridle Path Only", and follow this westwards under the impressive Croxdale Viaduct. After 880 yards, there is a kissing gate in the fence on your left which offers a shorter route along the riverside to Page Bank, where it joins the main route.

Continuing uphill, turn left past Holywell Hall where St Cuthbert's body is said to have rested on its travels. Another 880 yards uphill, turn right into Scripton Lane and follow this for over a mile, via Tudhoe Lodge to reach the A690. There are some fine backward views. Turn left to Scripton, a 19th century estate farmhouse. Here cross the A690 to the gate opposite and walk up to the Brandon/Bishop Auckland Walk.

Walk westwards along the track for 1½ miles to Brancepeth Station, noting on the way the views of Kirk Merrington Church and the beautiful Brancepeth Castle and church. Continue on and you will cross the wooded Stockley Gill. One and a half miles further on, before you approach Willington Industrial Estate, go through an open gap in the facing fence with a nearby bench seat and turn left down the unsignposted track to cross the busy A690 road. Thirty yards along this road in the direction of Brancepeth, turn right down an unsignposted enclosed lane.

You will pass by Willington's old brick and tip works. Further on down this byway, pass a grim cluster of buildings. At the junction of the lanes, you can go through the facing grey metal gate and down the field edge to the River Wear for a riverside ramble to Page Bank or turn left through the metal gate on your left and follow the byway eastwards for 1½ miles.

Where the track divides, turn left uphill for a steep walk past the four terraced cottages of Page Bank East and out on to Whitworth Lane. Turn right down this busy road to Page Bank. Cross Page Bank Bridge over the River Wear and walk up the steep Whitworth Road for half a mile to pass the entrance of Whitworth Hall, totally rebuilt in 1877 after a fire. This was the ancestral home of the famous Shafto family, where Bobby Shafto lived.

Yards up the road by Whitworth Hall Garden entrance, turn left through the Public Footpath signposted "kissing gate." Continue through a clump of trees and follow along and round by the high garden wall and then hug the fence on your left to exit through another kissing gate. Turn right and right again into a fenced path with a line of small oak trees.

Follow this eastwards via a couple of kissing gates into a narrow strip of woodland called Black Wood Plantation with its Nature Reserve. Go right along the surfaced lane and out of the wood, then eastwards along an enclosed lane. Skirt the new housing development of Spennymoor as well as the Rosa Shafto Nature Reserve and follow a well laid out path (logged on either side) down into the Valley Burn. Over the footbridge and out of the burn, climb up to the entrance of the sewage works, then right along a country lane.

From the crossroads, turn left and in yards cross a stile by a gate on your right and follow the fenced path with good views of Brancepeth Castle to the north. Go down the stiled fields to join the cart track from Coldstream Farm and turn right for a few yards and then along the wooded field edge to enter Coldstream Wood.

Head down the woodland footpath for a very muddy walk. On the sharp hill edge, descend steeply out of the wood, cross the footbridge over Nickynack Beck and follow the beckside path with the wood on your right. Join the riverside path which leads you under Croxdale Viaduct and along by the sewage works back to Sunderland Bridge.

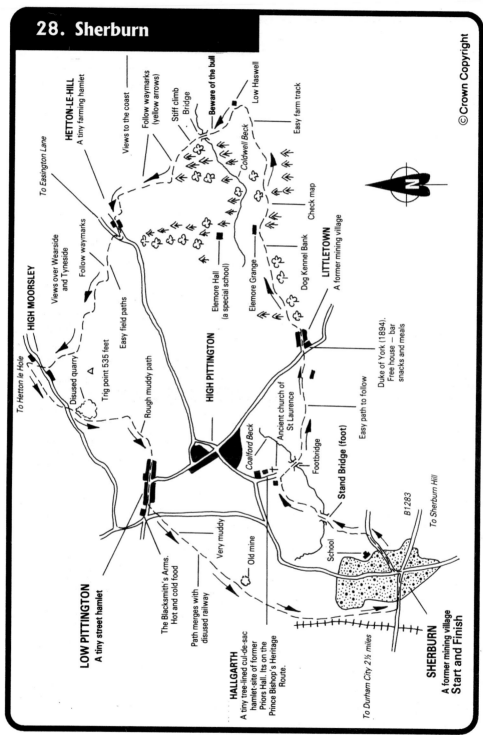

©Crown Copyright

HETTON-LE-HILL
A tiny farming hamlet

To Easington Lane

Views to the coast

Follow waymarks
(yellow arrows)

Stiff climb

Bridge

Beware of the bull

Low Haswell

Easy farm track

Coldwell Beck

Check map

HIGH MOORSLEY

Views over Wearside
and Tyneside

Follow waymarks

Easy field paths

Elemore Hall
(a special school)

Elemore Grange

Dog Kennel Bank

LITTLETOWN
A former mining village

To Hetton le Hole

Disused quarry

Trig point 535 feet

Rough muddy path

HIGH PITTINGTON

Ancient church of
St Laurence

Coalford Beck

Footbridge

Stand Bridge (foot)

Easy path to follow

Duke of York (1894).
Free house — bar
snacks and meals

LOW PITTINGTON
A tiny street hamlet

The Blacksmith's Arms.
Hot and cold food

Very muddy

Old mine

Path merges with
disused railway

School

B1283

To Sherburn Hill

HALLGARTH
A tiny tree-lined cul-de-sac
hamlet-site of former
Priors Hall. Its on the
Prince Bishop's Heritage
Route.

To Durham City 2½ miles

SHERBURN
A former mining village
Start and Finish

124

28. Sherburn

Route: Sherburn — Hallgarth — Littletown — Low Haswell — Hetton le Hill — High Moorsley — Pittington — Sherburn.
Distance: Under 9 miles (14.5km). Moderate. Field and woodland paths with a couple of stiff climbs.
O.S. Maps: Landranger Sheet 88. Pathfinder Sheet NZ 24/34.
Parking: Limited roadside parking in Sherburn.
Public Transport: United: Services 240, 241, 242, 244, X40, 60, 64. Durham City to Sherburn.
Refreshments: The Squire Trelawny Restaurant; Grey Horse and Cross Keys Sherburn; Duke of York, Littletown; The Blacksmith's Arms, Low Pittington.

This miners' meander is a splendid walk linking the villages of Sherburn with Littletown and Pittington in the former colliery country of East Durham. It offers fine views of five counties on a clear day including the Cleveland Hills and the Cheviots, plus the Pennines.

Leave Sherburn by the Pittington road. Almost opposite the George Parkinson Memorial Homes (1913), turn right along Hall Gardens, Nelson Terrace and Parkhouse Gardens to pass Sherburn Junior School. Follow the road out into the Durham countryside and turn left through the double metal gates at the end of the school playing fields. Follow the path between the ploughed field and go downhill to Coldwell Beck.

At the bottom, turn right along the rough beckside path, cross the metal footbridge called Stand Bridge and over the brow of a hill on a wide path to cross a large corner stile. Turn half right and follow the path which curves round and up to the tiny cul-de-sac hamlet of Hallgarth, the site of the former Priors' Hall, one of the places connected with the Prince Bishops of Durham.

The ancient church of St Laurence needs a visit even just to see the ten gravestones of the Baker-Baker family. Outside the churchyard, turn left down the enclosed path, cross the bridge and follow the field edge path to Littletown Farm to reach three terraced houses. Pass these, walk straight on up to the lane end and go through a kissing gate to follow the path, half left uphill to the top of the field.

Go through another kissing gate and along the sandy track to the Pittington road to come out opposite the former colliery village of Littletown which once had four pits. Cross the busy road to the popular pub called the Duke of York built in 1894. If you need refreshments (meals and snacks) owners Ian and Christine Walker give walkers a warm welcome. It's a popular spot with ramblers from Tyne and Wear.

From the pub walk along Plantation Avenue, bear left between the garages, cross a waymarked stile and go down the rough scrubland. Over the railed bridge, through a white gate and turn left into Dog Kennel Wood with a yellow waymark fixed to a tree pointing the direction along the rutted, muddy track below Dog Kennel Bank. Follow the track just inside the wood to pass between the stone gate pillars into the grounds of Elemore Hall. This brick-built, three-storey building was once the home of the Baker-Baker family and Anne Isabelle Milbank, born 1792, who married the poet Lord Byron. The hall is now a county council special school.

The route leads you down past the former farm buildings of Elemore Grange, a reminder of bygone days. Pass a "Two Mile" sign and the track dips down to the junction of three paths within the wood. Check the map, ignore the first path on your right and once over the beck also ignore the one on your left, but take the second on your right (waymark missing) for a steady climb up the narrow winding path by the beck and between the pines, planted to produce pit props. At the top, leave the wood, exit over a stile and pass a large circular water trough which used to be part of a stationary steam engine boiler. Keep by the wood/field edge and turn left up the sandy, gated track for a stiff climb to Low Haswell Farm with all-round views of the Durham countryside, including a couple of coastal collieries. At the top, just before the farm, cross a stile by a green gate, where you can stride from stile to stile.

Turn half right down the first field (very muddy) and drop steeply down the next two stiled fields with a warning in the second "Beware of the Bull". In the valley bottom, cross the concrete bridge and go over a stile into East Wood. Turn right and in yards, turn left up the wood for the steepest climb on the walk. Emerge out of the wood, over a stile and keep straight on along the path by the wood to go through a large gap. Here turn right and follow the farm track (waymarks vandalised) to Hetton le Hill with views of Tyneside and Wearside, plus popular Penshaw Monument.

Turn left along this tiny farming hamlet and by Bramble House, turn right along the road for 50 yards to enter the Borough of Sunderland, as well as Tyne and Wear. Cross the signposted stile on your left and follow the path which becomes a track by the fenced field edge. At the open field gap, ignore the waymarked stile on your left and turn

(Continued on page 126)

(Continued from page 125)

right up the field, fence on your right, and follow the waymarked path which swings left, westwards and upwards (500ft) along the field edge, giving fine views over five counties. The waymarked route leads you down into High Moorsley. Cross the busy road, take the signposted stile by the postbox/33, Valley View and descend the hillside path, where at the bottom turn left along the level path that leads you up to the Pittington road. Opposite, cross the signposted stile and follow the path upwards over the edge of Pittington Hill and onwards past an extensive disused quarry. From this lofty spot, admire the views as you walk along a level path (fence on your right) back into County Durham with views of Low Pittington.

Cross a stile and in yards turn right over another stile for a slippery descent down the bushy hillside, where the path levels out onwards, constantly check the map for an enclosed path via a kissing gate, on your right, that leads you down to a "Private Road Footpath Only" into Low Pittington. Turn right along the Front Street to the Blacksmiths Arms (hot and cold food) and turn left along the Sherburn road for a short distance and go through an unsignposted wooden gate on your right (check map) for the last leg of the walk.

Follow the level gated path, which after 880 yards merges with the popular rail trail that passes through the rubble remains of an old mine and 880 yards further on, as you approach a railway bridge, curve left uphill and walk parallel to the railway line and follow this southwards until the path veers left through a white gate for a return back to Sherburn.

29. Low Prudhoe

Route: Low Prudhoe — Ovingham — Ovington — Bywell — Stocksfield — Bullion Hills — Eltringham — Low Prudhoe
Distance: 7 miles (12.8km) Moderate. Allow 3/3½ hours.
O.S.Maps: Landranger Sheet 88. Pathfinder Sheet NZ 06/16
Parking: Tyne Riverside Country Park, Park Centre, Low Prudhoe. G.R. 086635. Car park south of Ovingham road bridge.
Public Transport: Northumbria Motor Services. Service 604. Newcastle — Prudhoe. British Rail — Newcastle — Low Prudhoe — Carlisle.
Refreshments: The Adam and Eve, Low Prudhoe; White Swan, The Bridge End Inn, Ovingham; Ship Inn, Highlander Inn, Ovington.

This walk explores East Tynedale on both sides of the River Tyne and links the villages of Ovingham with Ovington and Stocksfield with Low Prudhoe. It includes an interesting extension to bygone Bywell, one of the best bits of beautiful old Northumberland, where nothing now remains of the ancient Bywell village, except for two churches, a castle, a hall and a medieval market cross.

Leave Low Prudhoe car park and cross Ovingham Bridge over the River Tyne to the pleasant riverside village of Ovingham. Turn left and pass the Church of St Mary The Virgin which boasts the tallest and largest Saxon tower in Northumberland. The church is the burial place of Thomas Bewick, Northumbria's greatest artist, wood engraver and naturalist. At the west end of the village, cross the 17th century packhorse bridge and turn left over the green and follow the track by the Whittle Burn to reach the River Tyne. Turn right and follow the riverside path for 880 yards until you reach the holiday chalets. Leave the river, turn right and follow the track between the chalets and up through the fields to come out at the junction of the Ovington and Bywell roads.

Turn up the narrow road (no pavement) to the hillside village of Ovington and watch out for fast traffic. Go along the main street, where refeshments can be obtained from either the Ship Inn or the Highlander Inn, the latter an old coaching inn. Beyond the Highlander Inn, turn down the road called Burnside and at the far right hand corner, cross the stile signposted "Bywell 1½ miles" and admire the views over the Tyne Valley.

Go diagonally down the field and cross the stile at the bottom far right hand corner. Turn right along the field and go down to cross the half-hidden white painted stiled footbridge over the stream. Go half left up and along the hillock with fine views to go through a facing gate in the wire fence/broken wall. Continue in the same direction and go downhill to cross a step stile, left of a gate. Go straight over the centre of the next field, cross a stile and aim half left along the field, where yards from the field corner, cross the concealed dilapidated ladder stile on your left. Walk straight on over the field to cross the high ladder stile and exit out on to the busy riverside road. Turn right

The 13th century Bywell Cross

along the road with the River Tyne your companion to reach Bywell Bridge with the B6309 Stocksfield-Stamfordham road, where on summer weekends, you might be lucky to buy an ice cream.

Walkers wishing to visit the interesting village of Bywell should cross the road and in yards, go through the kissing gate signposted "Bywell" and follow the paddock path to come out at Bywell Castle, a 15th century tower gatehouse, where Henry VI took refuge after the Battle of Hexham in 1464. The castle is private and not open to the public. Turn left along the cul de sac road to the village of Bywell and see the 13th century Bywell Cross, a medieval market cross repositioned opposite the entrance to Bywell Hall. You must visit the twin churches of St Peter and St Andrew, the latter now redundant.

For the main route, return and cross Bywell Bridge over the River Tyne and follow the B6309 to Stocksfield, using a short cut via Stocksfield Station to come out by the Station Veterinary Clinic, opposite Stocksfield Post Office. Turn left and follow the A695 for 440 yards to pass Stocksfield Cricket Club and before you reach Merry Shield

(Continued on page 129)

© Crown Copyright

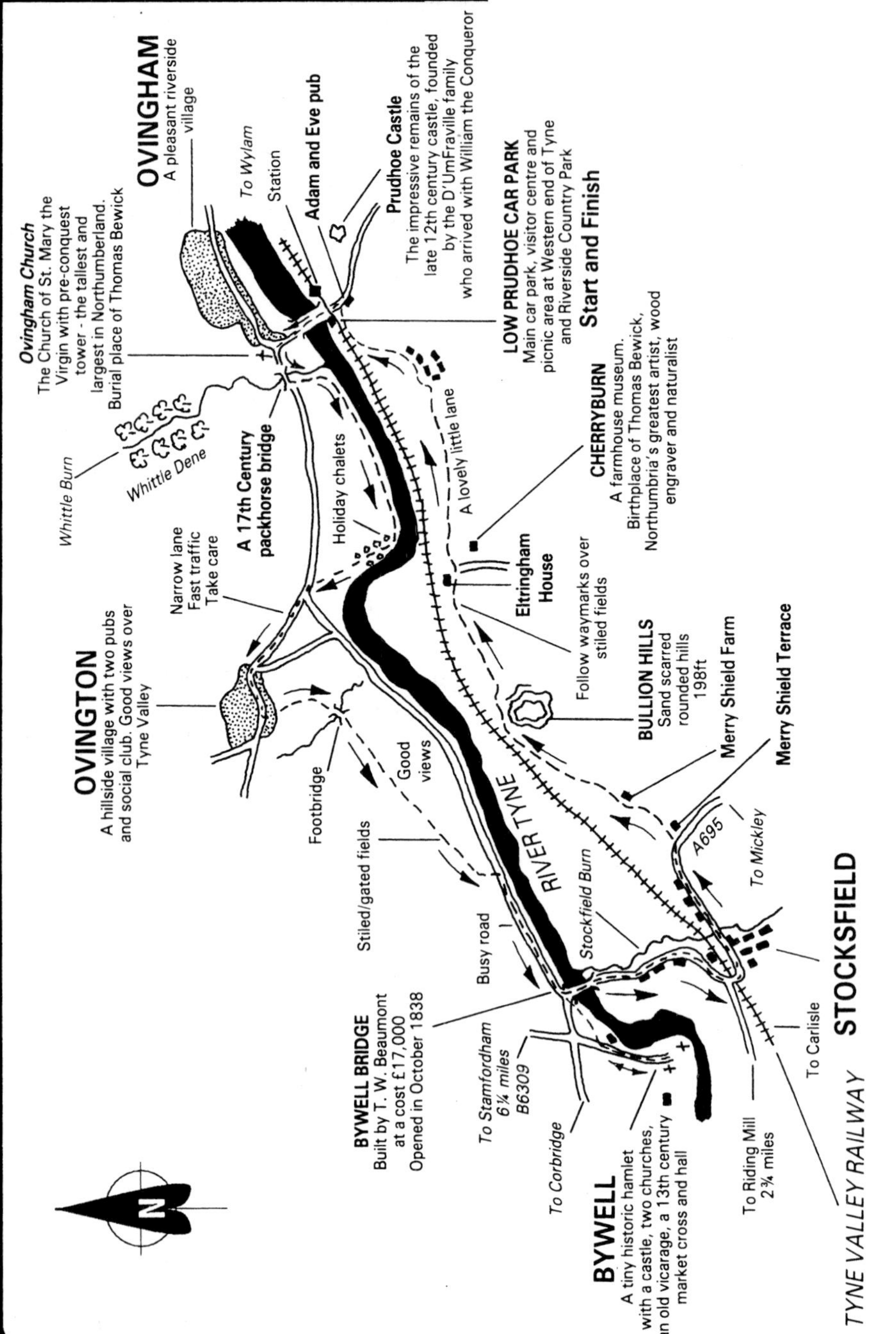

OVINGHAM
A pleasant riverside village

Ovingham Church
The Church of St. Mary the Virgin with pre-conquest tower - the tallest and largest in Northumberland. Burial place of Thomas Bewick

To Wylam

Station

Adam and Eve pub

Prudhoe Castle
The impressive remains of the late 12th century castle, founded by the D'UmFraville family who arrived with William the Conqueror

LOW PRUDHOE CAR PARK
Main car park, visitor centre and picnic area at Western end of Tyne and Riverside Country Park
Start and Finish

Whittle Burn

Whittle Dene

A 17th Century packhorse bridge

Holiday chalets

A lovely little lane

CHERRYBURN
A farmhouse museum, Birthplace of Thomas Bewick, Northumbria's greatest artist, wood engraver and naturalist

Narrow lane
Fast traffic
Take care

Eltringham House

Follow waymarks over stiled fields

OVINGTON
A hillside village with two pubs and social club. Good views over Tyne Valley

BULLION HILLS
Sand scarred rounded hills 198ft

Merry Shield Farm

Merry Shield Terrace

Footbridge

Good views

Stiled/gated fields

RIVER TYNE

A695

To Mickley

STOCKSFIELD

Stockfield Burn

Busy road

BYWELL BRIDGE
Built by T. W. Beaumont at a cost £17,000 Opened in October 1838

To Stamfordham 6¼ miles
B6309

To Corbridge

To Carlisle

To Riding Mill 2¾ miles

BYWELL
A tiny historic hamlet with a castle, two churches, an old vicarage, a 13th century market cross and hall

TYNE VALLEY RAILWAY

N

(Continued from page 127)

Terrace, turn left at the entrance sign of Merryshield Gravel Co. Ltd. and follow the lane to pass in front of Merry Shield Farm. Go down the track and where it turns right, walk straight on along the grass path and through a rusty gate into the bushy woodland. Follow the path straight ahead, cross a stile and continue along by the old spoil heaps covered with trees and bushes. The stiled path steadily climbs and levels out along by some Silver Birch trees.

Go through a facing wooden gate and immediately cross a waymarked stile in the fence on your right. Bear half left and climb the sandy slopes of Bullion Hills, where the path contours round the brow of the hill with glorious views of the Tyne Valley from Ovington to Ovingham.

Cross a waymarked ladder stile on your left and walk forward along the field edge with growing crops and cross a further ladder stile. Turn right for a few yards and on your left, cross another ladder stile by a gate. Follow the track over the brow of the short hill and aim through a white gate with the elegant Eltringham House away to your left. Go down the short farm driveway to the road. Here there is an interesting detour for those who

wish to step back in time and see Thomas Bewick's Cherryburn, the birthplace of Northumbria's great artist, wood engraver and naturalist. If so, turn right for a short steep climb up to Cherryburn and see the birthplace cottage, farm, plus printing house. It's well worth a visit.

Return down the road and 100 yards further on, with the rear of Eltringham House Farm on your left, turn right at the B&B sign and go up the unsurfaced mile-long little lane that heads eastwards and levels out giving good views across the Tyne Valley. You come out at Hunting Specialists Products Ltd and turn right up the road for a few yards and left along the unsurfaced path by the paint factory perimeter fence. Keep on this which becomes a tarmac path by the new houses of the Masters Close Estate. Go between two houses into Lime Grove, (if in doubt ask a local the way), turn down the cul de sac and go between the houses numbered 12 and 13 to turn right to reach a hillside stile overlooking the Tyne Valley. Go diagonally down the hillside and exit over a final stile and turn right through the factory units to come out by the Adam and Eve pub which deserves a visit. Turn left and return to Low Prudhoe car park to complete a satisfactory Tynedale circuit.

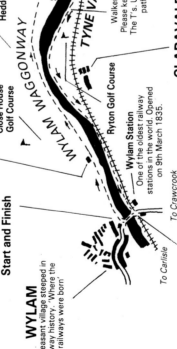

TYNE RIVERSIDE COUNTRY PARK
Riverside area: Open area of grassland with picnic tables and children's play equipment, overlooking boat ramp.

Newburn Visitor Centre
Call in for details on guided walks and events

Newburn Riverside Sports Centre

NEWBURN
An industrial suburb

THE BOATHOUSE INN
A popular riverside pub with dated flood levels

RIVER TYNE

To Blaydon

Newburn Bridge

THE TYNE VALLEY RAILWAY
One of Britain's oldest railways. The Newcastle—Carlisle railway opened in 1836.

To Newcastle

WYLAM WAGGONWAY
The waggonway was built around 1748 to transport coal from Wylam to the keels at Lemington. Part of the route has been opened as a public bridleway.

TYNE AND WEAR

Blayney Row (1889)
Terrace of former miners' cottages.

Reigh Burn

Ferry House

RYTON WILLOWS
A flat grassland riverside

GATESHEAD DISTRICT

Grange Road

Walkers— Please keep off The T's. Use the path

Heddon Haughs

Station House

HIGH STREET HOUSE
Small stone cottage built about 1750. Birthplace in 1781 of George Stephenson. The cottage is owned by the National Trust.

WYLAM WAGGONWAY

Close House Golf Course

CLARAVALE
Terraces of former miners' cottages. The colliery closed in 1960.

TYNE VALLEY RAILWAY

Ryton Golf Course

Wylam Station
One of the oldest railway stations in the world. Opened on 9th March 1835.

To Crawcrook

NORTHUMBERLAND

Wylam car park
Start and Finish

WYLAM
A pleasant village steeped in railway history. 'Where the railways were born'

Wylam Bridge
Built in 1836. Acquired by Northumberland County Council and freed from tolls on 2nd December 1936. Suffered extensive flood damage in January 1957 Renewed and widened in 1960.

To Carlisle

N

30. Wylam

Route: *Wylam — Blayney Row — Newburn Bridge — Ryton Willows — Ryton Golf Course — Wylam.*
Distance: *6 miles (9.5.km). Easy. Allow 3 hours.*
O.S. Maps: *Landranger Sheet 88. Pathfinder Sheet NZ 06/16.*
Parking: *Wylam Car Park in the former North Station Yard. Located behind Stephenson Terrace, on the north side of Wylam Bridge.*
Public Transport: *O.K Travel Service 684 Newcastle via Wylam — Ovington. British Rail — Newcastle-Hexham-Carlisle.*
Refreshments: *Pubs in Wylam. Wylam Teashop. The Boathouse Inn, West Row, Newburn.*

This pleasant riverside ramble on both sides of the River Tyne explores the Tyne Valley from Wylam to Newburn Bridge and returns along the south bank of the river. This easy-to-follow, low-level walk is suitable for anyone and recommended for any time of the year.

From Wylam car park, walk eastwards along the old railway track, now a bridleway, following the route of the Wylam Waggonway where famous locomotives such as Puffing Billy and Wylam Dilly first steamed along the Tyne Valley. The waggonway was built in 1748 to transport coal from Wylam Colliery to the keels at Lemington. It closed in 1867, when mining ceased at Wylam Colliery.

After half-a-mile, you will reach High Street House, better known as Stephenson's Cottage, where George Stephenson, 'The Father of Railways' was born on the June 9, 1781. The cottage is owned by the National Trust and open to the public. It is interesting to note that the first two miles of this walk is in the county of Northumberland including High Street House.

Further on, pass Close House Golf Course where pedestrians must exercise caution near the fairways. Follow the pleasant landscaped walkway with wild flowers in profusion and after a mile pass Heddon Haughs Farm on your left with the former stationmaster's house opposite, a reminder that this was Heddon Station which closed in 1958.

Continue on the public walkway and on the way, you can see the 120ft spire of the Holy Cross Church of Ryton towering above the trees across the Tyne, while eastwards is industrial Tyneside. In half a mile, pass the terrace cottages of Blayney Row (dated 1889) built to house employees of the Isabella Colliery situated behind Blaney Row. The colliery, opened in 1869 and closed in 1954, has been demolished and the site reclaimed. Beyond Blaney Row, follow the paved footpath on the north side of Grange Road and when you see the car park signs, cross the road

and turn left into the Tyne Riverside Country Park at Newburn. This was once an area of industrial dereliction, but with extensive reclamation schemes, the eyesores have been removed and transformed into a pleasant riverside park for all Tynesiders to enjoy. It includes picnic tables, play area and slipway as well as a Visitor Centre which will provide details of guided walks and events in the country park.

From the centre, take the riverside path, cross the footbridge over Reigh Beck and walk by the River Tyne to pass the playing fields of Newburn Riverside Sports Centre. Continue to the popular riverside pub called The Boathouse at West Row, an ideal halfway house for refreshments. This interesting pub has dated flood levels recorded on the pub wall - "The Great Flood 1771" — as well as the plaque to George Stephenson.

Cross Newburn Bridge over the River Tyne giving views of Tyneside's industrial landscape including the Stella Power Stations and the cone of the Northumberland Glass Works. At the bridge end, turn right down the steps and follow the riverside walk by the popular 54-acre flat grasslands of Ryton Willows flowered with gorse and broom bushes. Pass in front of Ferry House, where across the Tyne, you can see the ruined jetty of the old Ryton Ferry. Beyond Ferry House, the route runs parallel to the Tyne Valley Line — the Newcastle-Carlisle Railway — and the peace of this lovely walk is disturbed by diesel whistles and air traffic from Newcastle Airport.

Further on, the riverside path runs by Ryton Golf Course, where you are requested to keep to the paths and not venture on the golf links. Beyond the golf course the path cuts away from the riverside and follows the fenced path by the railway to exit into Wylam Station car park. The station built in 1835 is one of the oldest in the world. Cross Wylam Bridge, built in 1836 with nine spans of 40ft to return to Wylam car park to complete a satisfactory stroll in the Tyne Valley.

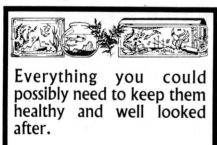

132

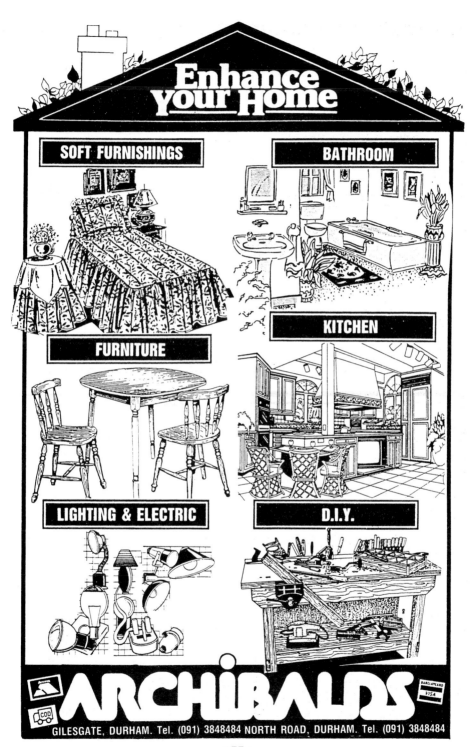

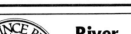

Step out on Kielder's self-guided walks!

Whether you're a keen walker or just like a leisurely stroll, you'll love walking at Kielder! We have developed seven different trails for you to enjoy.

See the Romano-British settlement on the Tower Knowe route; the eighteenth century beech trees on Leaplish's Beech Walk; the famous Kielder skew-arch viaduct on the Bakethin North Shore, and the peaceful wooded peninsula around the Belling area.

Our way-marked walks are beautifully described and illustrated in these leaflets available at Tower Knowe and Leaplish Waterside Park, priced 15p.

While you're at Kielder Water, there's plenty more to do ... boardsailing, cycling, fishing, ferry cruising, boating, nature watching ... whatever your interest, you'll love Kielder!

Kielder Water

Northumberland
Tel: (Information Centre) Bellingham (0434) 240398

Maintaining Your Feet Correctly is Essential to the Walker

Not only for the feet themselves, but to reduce effects of wear and tear on other joints e.g. ankles, knees, hips and back.

Visit a State Registered Chiropodist for advice or prevention of foot ailments as well as treatment of existing problems.

Most State Registered Chiropodists can prescribe and provide individual appliances and Orthotics to compensate for structural imbalance affecting the function of feet and legs.

Brotherton G.R. and Steven S.W. Mchs
NORWOOD HOUSE, WEST AVENUE, GOSFORTH. Tyneside 2843985

D. Darke Mchs
250 FULWELL ROAD, SUNDERLAND, WEARSIDE. Wearside 5493696

Dow A.H. & Savage
1ST FLOOR, 10, BIGG MARKET, NEWCASTLE. Tyneside 2325896

Dow A.N. Mchs
93 CHILLINGHAM ROAD, HEATON. Tyneside 2650295

Grant C. Mchs
36 RENWICK ROAD, BLYTH. Blyth 352053
FAWCETT HOUSE FAWCETT YARD, MORPETH. Morpeth 513205

Haddock A. Mchs
97 STATION ROAD, FOREST HALL. Tyneside 2150800

Henderson C.M. Mchs Srch
20 THE OVAL, BEDLINGTON. Bedlington 822017

Holmes S.M. Mchs Srch
5 DENE AVENUE, ROWLANDS GILL. Rowlands Gill 543910

Morrison C.H. Mchs
1 HOLMLANDS PARK, CHESTER-LE-STREET. Durham 388319

Pattison R. Mchs
5 BEATRICE TERRACE, SHINEY ROW. Durham 38533?

Pearson B. Mchs
176 SUNDERLAND ROAD, SOUTH SHIELDS. Tyneside 4556089

Powell J. Dpodm Mchs A. Gilchrist Bsc (Hons) Dpodm Mchs
36 ESLINGTON TERRACE, JESMOND. Tyneside 2811755

Savage P. Mchs
9 WESTERN HILL, NEAR ROYALTY, SUNDERLAND. Wearside 567347

Skilling W. Mchs
49 JOHN STREET, SUNDERLAND. Wearside 5655125

Teasdale J. Mchs
25 BURSWELL AVENUE, HEXHAM. Hexham 608612

Wilson G. Mchs
12 TWEED STREET, BERWICK. Berwick 306138

Look After Your Feet — There The Only Pair You Get Remember — when your feet hurt, you do hurt all over!

B.B. PROMOTIONS
(MARKETS)

SPECTACULAR

SUNDAY MARKET
AT
CATTERICK RACECOURSE

Open 10 a.m. - 4 p.m.

Over 200 stalls with 1000's bargains

FREE PARKING

Toilets/Facilities

FACILITIES FOR DISABLED

Refreshments/Hot Food

TOP QUALITY BUTCHER (Picher)

Why not make a day of it and visit historic Richmond and the surrounding areas.

46   070

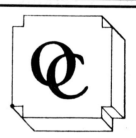

DURHAM
MILLBURNGATE
S H O P P I N G   C E N T R E

MORE SHOPS ...
MORE CHOICE ...
MORE COMFORT ...
MORE STYLE ...

Enjoy a day out combining excellent shopping facilities with a visit to the Historic Cathedral and Castle

Some of the Retail Names in the Centre are:-

T & G Allan

Dorothy Perkins

Dixons

Early Learning Centre

Evans

Fosters

Holland & Barrett

Mothercare

Monument Sports

Safeway

Principles

Rumbelows

Our Price Records

PLUS MANY MORE

Come and shop in pleasant surroundings free from traffic and the weather, with under cover parking available for over 500 cars.

An Experience to Remember.
The Millburngate Shopping Centre is managed by the British Coal Pension Funds.

MILLBURNGATE SHOPPING CENTRE, FRAMWELLGATE AND MILLBURNGATE BRIDGES, DURHAM.

Index